To God's Glory

To God's Glory

The Art of Servanthood
Discipleship

Isaac Benjamin-Nyarko

Jesus Joy Publishing

Published and printed in Great Britain in 2016 by
Jesus Joy Publishing.

© Isaac Benjamin-Nyarko, 2016

All rights reserved. The author gives permission for brief extracts from this book to be used in other publications provided that the following citation is stated:
Extract from 'The Art of Servanthood Part One - Discipleship' by Isaac Benjamn-Nyarko, 2016; Jesus Joy Publishing used by permission.

Unless otherwise indicated, all scripture quotations are taken from the New King James Version. Copyright © 1979, 1980, 1982 by Thomas Nelson, Inc. Used by permission. All rights reserved.

Scripture quotations noted KJV are taken from King James Version. 1611 original, 1769 revision. Crown Copyright.

ISBN 978-1-90797-142-6

Jesus Joy Publishing
is a division of Eklegein Ltd
www.jesusjoypublishing.co.uk
20160401

Dedication

I dedicate this book to His most Excellency, Jesus Christ, who is my Lord and Saviour as well as the King of kings and the Lord of Lords. I thank God for His goodness and all the wonderful things He faithfully continues to do in my life. Though I do not deserve His grace, I am privileged and overjoyed to be a chosen vessel of God.

There is nothing more precious in life than the Salvation of Christ. Without Jesus, I would have no reason to live. I do not know where I would be without the Lord. All glory and honour belong to the Almighty God, the supreme and the immutable King who lives forever.

Acknowledgements

A very big thank you to all those who supported me in prayer when circumstances threw me down to zero. They were the angels of the Lord in human form. They really held me up so that I did not dash my feet against the stones the enemy laid before me. God bless them forever.

My sincere gratitude to the very few individuals who believed in my dream and helped me to bring this book to life. It has been a long and hard journey, but by the grace of God, I am grateful to have come this far.

A special thanks my father, J.M.Adade Nyarko and my family. God bless them all abundantly.

I give glory to God for the great men and women of God in my life who function as bishops, apostles, prophets, teachers and mentors; I salute them for the phenomenal impact they have made in my life so far. May all the blessings in Heaven be released into their lives until Jesus comes back again.

Contents

Dedication	7
Acknowledgements	9
Preface	13
Discipline Prevents Chaos	19
Reliance On The Word	39
Obedience And Disobedience	57
The Effects Of The Past	77
Efficiency And Effectiveness	95
Use Your Talents To Build God's Kingdom	115
The Power To Overcome	141
Prudence	153
Final Word	163
Also By The Author	165

Preface

In my lifetime, my eyes have witnessed many people fall from great heights and others rise from abysmal lows. For many years, I have wondered why some individuals were able to reach the top and why others fell to the bottom. What was the key to the success of those who rose to great heights, and what caused the downfall of those who were unable to make it to the top?

Growing up, I noticed that many people failed to achieve their goals in positive ways because of ungodly decisions. Over the years, I have observed Christians in colossal positions come short of fulfilling their purpose as a result of the choices they make. I have come to the conclusion that there are still many Christians who lack the right understanding to achieve their goals. Some are aware of their weaknesses, but are too complacent to do something about them. They do not allow Christ to have an impact in their lives. Some cannot understand it, and it has caused them to focus on contrary things instead. This is the attitude that is causing many believers to take the wrong directions.

A very lamentable example of an individual who took the wrong direction was Samson, who allowed his lust for a Philistine woman to distract him. Even after that, he went further and entangled himself with another Philistine, Delilah, who led him into captivity. Samson lost all his strength because his infatuation with Delilah compelled him to reveal the secret of his power to her and she betrayed him. Once taken captive, Samson's eyeballs were plucked out by his enemies. However, his story arrives at a successful conclusion, since he did not allow the pain of his defeat to completely discourage him. Eventually, he fulfilled his destiny because he finally reached out to God before his heroic death. [Judges 16:28-30] Although Samson completed his assignment, he could have prevented his captivity and the loss of his eyes if only he had stayed away from the Philistine women.

There are so many situations in our lives that are symbolised by the 'Philistine women'. They are the influences that cause us to lose focus on our duties and in turn, produce catastrophes and disappointments. In some cases, these influences could be anger, bitterness, covetousness, or problems in marriage. In other cases, it could be laziness and other serious addictions like drugs, excessive eating, alcohol, pornography, overworking, or gambling. These can cause individuals to lose their way and fall into despair.

There are other types of 'philistine women' such as an extreme love for money or material wealth, which can cause us to make some very regrettable mistakes. They could also take the form of spending too much time in front of the television or in the company of friends whose influences are detrimental. The wrong turns we take can expose our weaknesses and can ruin a hard-earned reputation. It is important to be careful of the choices we make. In the extraordinary life of Samson, Delilah was the cause of his final downfall, but for many of us who are still alive, we may not know our limits. It may be too late for some who do not yet know when to quit. By this, I mean that, Samson only had the Philistine women to deal with, but in the lives of many of us today, it could be a combination of factors. Therefore, it is imperative to focus on the divine attributes of Christ in order to avoid these pitfalls. The wrong choices only produce failure and distress.

Lot's family was specifically warned; they were told not to look back at the destruction of Sodom and Gomorrah. But, Lot's wife could not resist the temptation to have a final glimpse of what she was leaving behind. She was turned into a pillar of salt because she chose to look back. Salt is good in many ways, but it also has a very bitter taste. It may also symbolise the bitterness and pain which wrong choices bring. Now, imagine what could have happened if the whole family had turned and looked back at the destruction of their past. As God caused fire and brimstone to rain upon Sodom and

Gomorrah, it was imperative for Lot and his family to stay focused. The desire to look back at the place they once lived could have wiped out a generation. There could have been more pillars of salt standing in the wilderness. Therefore, this comes as a counsel to warn us all who are privileged to be God's children - we need to be careful of the steps we take and the decisions we make in our lifetime.

Are your choices causing 'fire and brimstone' to rain upon your destiny? Are you making decisions that continue to turn your dreams and aspirations into pillars of bitterness?

By God's grace, you have a wonderful opportunity to make a complete change in your life, so that God will smile down on you. Through this book, I pray that you will begin to walk in the paths of righteousness and step into God's glory. Sometimes, we do not allow God to guide us because we often perceive that we can make it on our own. Some have relied on their academic qualifications and status more than on God. This shows that they have reverence for intellectual enlightenment more than the wisdom of God. Countless individuals have become more accustomed to the knowledge of man as a way to accumulate wealth and worldly admiration. As such, they have failed to accomplish their purpose in God. Many men and women have suffered curses because they chose to follow their own judgment according to the instructions of the world. Many individuals have had to endure frustration and affliction because they took the wrong turns by engaging in ungodly activities. On the other hand, some have blessings because they made the choice to trust in God and applied the principles of His Word. It is a great privilege to be guided by the Lord because He is infallible. As long as we follow in the footsteps of Christ, our Redeemer, we will surely fulfil our divine destinies.

Chapter One

Discipline Prevents Chaos

"Therefore take up the whole armour of God, that you may be able to withstand in the evil day, and having done all, to stand.

Stand therefore, having girded your waist with truth, having put on the breastplate of righteousness, and having shod your feet with the preparation of the gospel of peace; above all, taking the shield of faith with which you will be able to quench all the fiery darts of the wicked one.

And take the helmet of salvation, and the sword of the Spirit, which is the word of God; praying always with all prayer and supplication in the Spirit, being watchful to this end with all perseverance and supplication for all the saints."

[Ephesians 6:13-18]

Character Development

Discipline is the principal aspect of the lifestyle of a Disciple. Without discipline, a person cannot become a true servant of God. This principle helps us to appreciate the importance in doing things well and how to behave correctly. Furthermore, discipline is a contrivance that can enable an individual or a group of people to grow to become exceptional leader(s). It takes great responsibility to become an overseer of a person, a group, or perhaps, a nation. It certainly takes discipline to build the necessary character to conquer the seemingly unconquerable.

A man instructed his young son to dig a number of holes in their back garden in order to plant little trees. The man woke his son up very early every morning and the boy did his best to dig holes and plant trees. It was not long before he began to complain about the pains in his body. The boy's father nursed him until the pain was gone; then, he went back to digging more holes and planted more trees, but this time he worked without his father's supervision. Upon completing the job, he noticed that some of the trees had already begun to grow. His father sat him down and told him how proud he was of his diligent labour. The father also noticed how healthy and strong his son had become.

The digging of holes and the planting of trees was a process of development for the boy to gain some character and turn him into a responsible man. As painful and challenging as it was, his character building turned him into a mature adult– ready to compete in the world. After all his hard work, his father gave him a huge amount of land and many possessions - including a trust fund, which was saved up for him over the years. This proves that character-building certainly brings rewards. Ironically, there are individuals who often struggle to discipline themselves properly to perform their duties, because they are too reliant on supervision and they cannot stay focused when left to their own devices.

However, there are some who have the inner strength to discipline themselves properly - to make good decisions without any guidance at all. It is very beneficial to possess the ability to achieve results without the influence of external forces. [Proverbs 6:6-8] This does not mean that guidance is unnecessary. As a matter of fact, supervision is of paramount importance because, without it there would be no order and many would lack direction. However, it pays to have the ability to be self-reliant.

The Significance Of Growth

As children of the Almighty God, we are Spiritual Soldiers. We are fighting a war that cannot be seen by human eyes because the war is a spiritual battle. We have been called to be soldiers for Christ and God has equipped us with spiritual weapons to destroy the works of Satan. However, it is important that we receive the right training from the Lord, so that we will be effective warriors.

> *"For we do not wrestle against flesh and blood, but against principalities, against powers, against the rulers of the darkness of this age, against spiritual hosts of wickedness in the heavenly places."*
>
> [Ephesians 6:12]

Before individuals become soldiers, they undertake the correct type of training that shapes them into formidable warriors; their training experience is like a metamorphosis. For this reason, recruits change from ordinary to extraordinary people. This process enables them to change their values as they experience new things. This method of preparation enables them to attain the required character in order to endure well in the most challenging situations; their mentalities change as they mature, which helps to determine the decisions they make.

Likewise, when children are raised well, they learn to be responsible as they mature into adults. The choices of adults are obviously different from the choices of children who need constant attention and protection because they are not experienced enough.

The young are certainly not wise enough to make cogent decisions. Therefore, as children of the Lord, it is necessary that we all seek to renew our minds daily according to God's counsel. The way we think is what makes us who we are, but when we renew our minds, we become different people. However, let us see how this fits into our daily walk with Christ and why it is important that we learn to grow in the Lord.

> *"If indeed you have heard Him and have been taught by Him, as the truth is in Jesus: that you put off, concerning your former conduct, the old man which grows corrupt according to the deceitful lusts, and be renewed in the spirit of your mind, and that you put on the new man which was created according to God, in true righteousness*

and holiness."

[Ephesians 4:21-24]

As we mature in Christ, our minds experience a remarkable alteration, which in turn–motivates us to reject our earthly values and acknowledge the principles of God. Our values change as a result of the new character we gain in the Lord, which contributes to significant growth on our spiritual journey. Our new character focuses on the attributes of God; therefore, it is important that we learn to relinquish the old character in us. Our old character is known as 'the old man' and the new character is known as 'the new man' or 'the spirit man.' The old and new man, are both symbols of the past versus the present and the future. The old man represents the worldly life before we are born again, but the new man represents the new life that we receive after we have been made new in Christ. The spirit man also stands for the present life we live now in Christ and this new life determines our destiny. Moreover, our spirit man possesses the type of character that is capable of glorifying God because it is born of the Holy Spirit. [Galatians 2:18]

Question:

What do you think of most often - things that bring glory to God or things that only offend Him?

In order to understand how mature you are in Christ, it is important to identify who and what is governing, or has framed your mentality. This often depends on what you have been fixing your eyes on, who you have been paying attention to, and with whom you associate. Analyse yourself and estimate the percentage of ungodly thoughts compared to the godly thoughts which dominate your mind. This will help you to understand whether your values are detrimental or inspirational. Very often, we do not realise that some of our values can be damaging until something negative occurs. This is why it is important to renew our minds daily. [Romans 12:2]

New converts need to mature into diligent disciples because their natural character, which is the old man, does not display God's virtues. This is due to the fact that the old man contains characteristics that often satisfy the flesh. In addition, the old man is more susceptible to the suggestions of the devil. Let us be reminded again that the new man has a type of nature which glorifies God because he has been regenerated by the Spirit of God. [Ephesians 3:16]

> "If then you were raised with Christ, seek those things which are above, where Christ is, sitting at the right hand of God. Set your mind on things above, not on things on the earth. For you died, and your life is hidden with Christ in God. When Christ who is our life appears, then you also will appear with Him in glory. Therefore put to death your members which are on the earth: fornication, uncleanness, passion, evil desire, and covetousness, which is idolatry. Because of these things the wrath of God is coming upon the sons of disobedience, in which you yourselves once walked when you lived in them. But now you yourselves are to put off all these: anger, wrath, malice, blasphemy, filthy language out of your mouth."
>
> [Colossians 3:1-8]

As much as the spirit man is of God, the character still has to experience spiritual training through the Word of God in order to acquire all the attributes of Christ. New Christians are especially in need of such training because the spirit man is a new-born baby and needs to gain the necessary strength to overcome the power of the flesh. New-born babies must be well guided and educated by their parents or guardians until they are matured enough to govern their own lives. Likewise, a new trainee in the military has to be under expert authority in order to become a fully experienced soldier. In contrast, children of God are under the unique influence of Jesus Christ whose spiritual education transforms them daily from nothing to something, from weakness to strength, from darkness into light, from poverty into prosperity, from fear to faith, and from losers to champions. [2 Corinthians 5:17]

Levels of Maturity and Establishment

In the Military, there are numerous ranks, which can only be achieved through overcoming many challenging stages and experiences.

> *"You therefore must endure hardship as a good soldier of Jesus Christ. No one engaged in warfare entangles himself with the affairs of this life, that he may please him who enlisted him as a soldier."*
>
> [2 Timothy 2:3-4]

In the Bible, when Jesus called the disciples, they became His recruits. But, after He trained them for a period of time, He commissioned them to go out and spread the Gospel. For some, it takes only months, whilst for others, it takes several years of discipleship before they actually do the work of God.

In the military, there are non-commissioned officers and commissioned officers. [Matthew 28:19] The responsibility of a commissioned officer is to lead other troops as a unit commander in all types of situations. Therefore, as we grow in Christ, it is important to understand that we are commissioned to lead others out of the darkness of the world and into the light of God. Regardless of your skill, or your position in ministry, it is the duty of a Christian to disciple converts of God's Kingdom.

The responsibilities of officers increase as their ranks increase. As they gain more experience, they are expected to take on tougher roles as they move up the ladder. As a Disciple of Christ, it is paramount to learn all the basics first before you move up the ladder, one rung at a time. Do not rush, because every stage in your life has essential lessons that will equip you to become an effective leader. Through that, you will understand how to guide others from darkness into light and raise good leaders for the Kingdom.

God will promote you to the appropriate position when you are ready to handle a higher status in the Kingdom. So, as a child of God and a soldier for Christ, it is essential to learn all that you need to learn as you mature in the Lord.

We can only be effective teachers when we have studied to show ourselves approved by God. [2 Timothy 2:15]

> *"For though by this time you ought to be teachers, you need someone to teach you again the first principles of the oracles of God; and you have come to need milk and not solid food. For everyone who partakes only of milk is unskilled in the word of righteousness, for he is a babe. But solid food belongs to those who are of full age, that is, those who by reason of use have their senses exercised to discern both good and evil."*
>
> [Hebrews 5:12-14]

When those who have been believers for some time are only capable of what newborn babes can do, then it is a sign that they need to become mature in the Lord and strong enough to face greater challenges.

There are believers who appoint themselves to positions of authority. They also give themselves platforms and titles without going through the necessary stages. Ironically, there are believers who have been in the Lord for many years and they should be great leaders, but they are still at the lowest level because they refuse to humble themselves to be trained by other believers with more experience. Some already see themselves as Generals, but they do not even have what it takes to handle the most basic responsibilities.

Furthermore, those who see themselves as Generals often try to destroy the ones who are genuinely going through the correct stages of growth. New recruits do not have what it takes to handle the responsibilities of high-ranking officers, because they lack the expertise to be at that level.

Putting ourselves on pedestals and proclaiming great titles

will only expose us to catastrophe, especially when we have not genuinely earned the right nor fully gained the experience to handle the responsibilities of leadership; in doing so, we only open ourselves to defeat.

In life, there are important stages that are necessary to pass through. In doing so, we can acquire the very best of knowledge. The things we learn can equip us to accomplish our goals. Moreover, there are imperative trials and spiritual experiences that every child of God must endure in order to become like the Lord.

A baby is only able to drink and digest milk, but also has to be nurtured under the wise counsel of parents until that child reaches a certain age. Sometimes, the child has to come face to face with some opposition in order to teach the child to become strong. In the same way, new recruits in the military who have not yet had the harrowing experience of battle may never know what it is like until they face it.

Loyalty of the Saints

There are many powerful tasks and missions for soldiers to undertake, but one of the most important qualities for soldiers to display is loyalty. Before recruits join the army, they must enunciate and sign an oath of allegiance, which is a declaration of their commitment to service in the armed forces. The oath is proclaimed, as it is in a court of law to ensure that the individuals who pronounce the oath will abide by the regulations. As trainees are sworn into the army, new converts are also ushered into the Kingdom of God through the Word – a confession of faith in Jesus Christ.

> *"... if you confess with your mouth the LORD Jesus and believe in your heart that God has raised Him from the dead, you will be saved. For with the heart one believes unto righteousness, and with the mouth confession is made unto salvation. For the Scripture says,'Whoever believes on*

Him will not be put to shame.'"

[Romans 10:9-11]

As we give our lives to Christ, we make a vow to accept Him as our personal Lord and Saviour. This is another indication that Christ owns us because the word 'Lord' means 'Owner' or 'Overseer'. Therefore, as soon as we make that pledge, we acknowledge that Christ is our Master, Shepherd, Provider, and Protector. Nevertheless, this has to be by choice, as soldiers do not typically join the army forcefully; rather, they choose to enlist of their free will. Though, there are times that people are enlisted into the military by involuntary subscription. All the same, believers come into the Kingdom of God according to their own free will; God does not force anyone to become a Christian.

As much as we want the Lord to be our friend and supplier of all our needs, sometimes we want Him to take the back seat and allow us to captain our own lives - as if we know better. This is how we often fail to make the kind of progress we are supposed to make. It is essential to acknowledge that Christ has the expertise to be in charge because He never fails. As the Bible declares us as soldiers for Christ; it means we are the employees of the Lord. It is our duty to follow His orders and keep the enemy under our feet. It is essential to equip ourselves with everything that God gives us - in order to be fervent warriors of the Kingdom. When we fail to make Christ the Lord of our lives, we fail to show our loyalty to Him. [2 Timothy 2:3-4]

> *"Now as they sat and ate, Jesus said, 'Assuredly, I say to you, one of you who eats with Me will betray Me.' And they began to be sorrowful, and to say to Him one by one, 'Is it I?' And another said, 'Is it I?' He answered and said to them, 'It is one of the twelve, who dips with Me in the dish. The Son of Man indeed goes just as it is written of Him, but woe to that man by whom the Son of Man is betrayed! It would have been good for that man if he had*

never been born.'"

[Mark 14:18-2]

Loyalty is essential in every soldier; soldiers can fall into the hands of enemies especially if they allow their weaknesses to get in the way. It is important that soldiers remain fully obedient in service to their regiment. It is not acceptable for a soldier to be impulsive or to be afraid to fight because that can be a great catastrophe to a regiment and an entire army. That weakness can also affect a whole nation. Moreover loyalty can become a device for exploitation when the ones who occupy the greatest positions use their platforms as a weapon to suppress others. For example, king Saul used his position to bully his servant David. Eventually, David had to break away from Saul because he was abusive. As a matter of fact, Saul made several attempts to kill David because he envied him.

This is what often gives certain individuals the licence to disregard the importance of loyalty and instead embrace the attitude of rebellion. [2 Kings 2:1-14] There are believers who have lost the virtue of loyalty due to the disappointments they have experienced with other members of the congregation. Sometimes Christians move from church to church because they lose trust in the people they look up to.

Since I gave my life to Christ, I have come across believers who are unsure of the congregations in which they worship. Some could not remain in the same church, because they were disrespected by their pastors and other members of the church. Consequently, such individuals could not grow spiritually, and they lost their closeness with God. In many cases, Christians have been known to be disloyal to their church because they do not agree with the rules and regulations of the church. Though Judas was close to Jesus, he also associated with people who only wanted to destroy Jesus.

There are many reasons why believers cannot be loyal; some

of the reasons are very petty, and some of the reasons seem plausible. Nevertheless, it is important to worship the Lord in the right place with the right people. Jesus Christ did not abuse His power whilst He was on earth. Christ did not give His disciples a reason to be rebellious. This is because Jesus Himself also learned to be obedient in accordance with the Word of God. He had to study to show Himself approved as He grew into adulthood. [Luke 2:52]

Jesus experienced many things in life as He matured, but He never wavered from His calling. He epitomised the art of servanthood. God warns leaders against abusing their power by trampling on those whom they are called to serve. In the Kingdom of God, it is vital to give honour to others regardless of who you are and what you have achieved. When leaders exploit their servants, it opens the door for disloyalty. Therefore, the best ways to make loyalty more attractive to people is to maintain the conduct of love and respect. As believers in the Kingdom of God, we are required to love and honour each other because that is what edifies the body of Christ.

Endurance

Endurance is the ability to persevere. It is a capability that can help you to work hard. When you understand how endurance works, it can help you to maintain your determination–even in the most difficult times. Moreover, it is an attribute that can help you to resist all opposition - despite how overwhelming it may appear to be. One of the greatest aspects of a soldier's training in the military is to learn to endure. Soldiers never stop fighting for their cause - regardless of the intensity of predicaments they experience on the battlefield. Thus, it is important that we continue to stand strong in the Lord in spite of what comes against us.

One of the most important aspects of endurance is patience. It is the ability to wait until the correct time to hear from God against all odds. Sometimes we face many seemingly intolerable situations in our lives, but the competence to resist and overcome them is what's essential.

> *"But those who wait on the LORD shall renew their strength; they shall mount up with wings like eagles, they shall run and not be weary, they shall walk and not faint."*
> [Isaiah 40:31]

Endurance can be a very painful process, but it is a remarkable tool because it can empower an individual with the dexterity to reach an expected end. Therefore, be strong in the Lord and learn to endure 'till the very end, so that you will attain your prize. From time to time, God allows us to experience circumstances which often seem impossible and hopeless. However, God often uses such harrowing episodes in our lives to strengthen us so that we will produce positive testimonies to inspire others.

Let us take a look at the Almighty God and how He has been long-suffering towards us all. Despite our filthiness and all the evil we do in this world, God does not always complain to us about our behaviour. He restrains Himself from losing His patience with us.

In fact, God gave us the greatest solution to our sins and all our imperfections, because He loves us dearly. That perfect solution He gave us was Jesus Christ. This means that God has not yet given up on us and He will never lose sight of us. From the Biblical account of Jesus, we know that He could have chosen to give up when He realized the weight of the death He was going to experience on the Cross. Having all the sins of mankind placed on Him was extremely heavy; nevertheless, Christ did not complain to God or man. He did not point fingers at anybody, but He compliantly endured the immeasurable pain and shame on the Cross for our sake.

Similarly, God appointed Moses and equipped him to be the deliverer of the Israelites after spending forty years in the wilderness. The journey from Egypt to Israel through the desert lasted many years. It was a challenging responsibility for Moses because the children of Israel were often very stubborn.

There were times that it was almost as if Moses could not handle it anymore, but he still had to endure until he finished the job. If Moses had given up half way, it could have indeed been catastrophic. Only God knew the disaster that could have occurred if Moses had given up on his assignment. As a result of their high level of stubbornness, it was necessary for the people of Israel to experience the wilderness as a bridge to their Promised Land. [Exodus 32:9-14]

They had to learn to endure the harshness and the roughness of the deserts in order to be transformed. However, God had no choice but to kill most of them because they were rebellious. So, it was only the young ones who were able to enter into the Promised Land through the leadership of Joshua.

There are many renowned men and women of God who had to learn to appreciate the significance of endurance in order to become effective servants of the Lord. Frankly, anyone who does not understand the principle of endurance will struggle to succeed. Sometimes, frustration and bitterness can persuade us to push ourselves in the wrong direction. But when we understand how important endurance is, we will refuse to waver regardless of what we face. When things are not going well for us, impatience can cause us to act on impulse - to create a change to suit ourselves. The way we react to difficult situations can threaten our ability to fulfil our purpose; particularly, if our actions are not in line with God's will. Therefore, let us be reminded that we are called to be soldiers of Christ. It is imperative that we go through whatever we need to go through, so that we will gain the correct experience to accomplish our purpose in God.

Punctuality

Punctuality is an attitude of time-keeping, promptness, reliability, and availability. Timing is very crucial in the lives of soldiers; they must be punctual and their attendance must be consistent. Being on time and being ready to fulfil their duties is very important in the economy of God. It is important that soldiers are always on time and in their rightful place to fulfil the obligations they are assigned to. We know that God is always timely; He is never late-even when it appears as if He is. He always shows up at the right time - without fail. God is never too busy to visit us and He is never too busy to hear our prayers. Therefore, as children of God, it is needful to be as punctual and consistent as possible, because many lives and many destinies are depending on us. [John 11:32-33]

Jesus Christ was not late to Calvary; He was there on time and He died on the Cross at the right time. His crucifixion was exactly according to plan. Before His death on the Cross, the Lord declared that He would be resurrected three days after His death and that was exactly what happened. Christ did not stay dead for five days because it would have been too late and His death and resurrection would have been insignificant.

> *"For I delivered to you first of all that which I also received: that Christ died for our sins according to the Scriptures, and that He was buried, and that He rose again the third day according to the Scriptures, and that He was seen by Cephas, then by the twelve."*
> [1 Corinthians 15:3-5]

Lazarus died and had been in the tomb four days when Jesus arrived, from Martha's point of view, it looked as if it was too late. Nevertheless, the Lord saw things differently because He knew that He had the power to turn the seemingly impossible situation around. Though, it seemed as if there was no way that Lazarus could ever come back to life, Jesus showed up at the right time and raised him from the dead.

In the eyes of many, it looked like it was too late for anything good to happen, but in the eyes of the Lord, He was right on time. [John 11:17-26]

Sometimes, God will allow the situations in your life to get worse than they are, even to a point that it may appear as if there is absolutely nothing that can be done. This does not mean that God will allow the situations to devour you. Our God is the only one who has the absolute power to break through the most impenetrable things and restore everything back to life. God always shows up at the right time even when it seems as if He has forgotten us. There has never been, and there will never be a time that the Lord will be late for something or someone, or fail to show up at all. He never fails!

Time is paramount, because God works through it; He also works through seasons. [Ecclesiastes 3:1] There is a time to plant and a time to harvest; however, between the time of planting and harvest, there are times of waiting and labouring until the manifestation of fruitfulness. If God always showed up at the wrong time, the entire universe would be in total chaos. In the same manner, when we are late or fail to show up for an important assignment, it could result in serious consequences, which could take a lifetime to rectify.

Supernatural Intelligence

Soldiers have to develop a very high level of intelligence, which enables them to be several steps ahead of their enemies. Skilled military personnel have the expertise to exercise their senses; they can detect if something is poisonous by its smell or by its behaviour. They are also able to predict the level of toxicity in water by its colour, taste, or smell. Other skills include the ability to recognize something by the sound it makes, or being able to tell which direction the wind is blowing, and how far away something is by the way it sounds. As the Christian walk is like that of military men, we have a special role to play in this world because we are a special breed of people.

We are a unique nation because we are set aside to do the special work of the Lord. [Hebrews 5:14] It is important for a soldier to have the ability to read signs of danger or sense when something is wrong. These distinctive abilities give soldiers the opportunity to fully prepare for, and learn how to prevent potential threats. There are equipment such as radar, metal detectors, and other sensors, which soldiers use to check for possible danger. They are used to detect the plans of the enemy in advance before it is too late. In order for Christians to practice this act of precautionary detection, they have to be knowledgeable in the Word of God. As 'spiritual soldiers', there are also spiritual forces that battle against us daily; but, because they cannot be seen with the naked eye, many perceive them to be non-existent.

However, they are real and dangerous because they are capable of doing some unimaginable things. Nevertheless, we have the power to conquer them all. When Jesus went to pray on the Mount of Olives before His arrest, He specifically instructed His disciples to wait and watch, but they failed to comply. Jesus was not happy to see the disciples sleeping when He returned from His first prayer. Being on guard through prayer and fasting sharpens us spiritually; it helps us to focus and be ready for the unexpected, because there are many dangers that can take us by surprise. When you fail to be on guard and on the alert for potential danger, it is possible that you will fall into despair. God can reveal all the plans of the enemy to you by means of dreams, visions, prophecy, and through His Word or through a situation.

When we are sharpened in the spirit, we will be able to detect things in advance, and sense oncoming dangers so that we may avoid them quickly. This unique ability enables believers to be powerful, as it helps us to identify what unbelievers cannot comprehend.

Soldiers have the skill to defuse explosives; we all know what explosives can do. Therefore, it is imperative that Christians should also learn how to spiritually counteract situations before they blow up into catastrophes. [Matthew 26:41] In the Bible, we learn how Jesus Christ defused impossible situations and turned bad conditions into good ones. There are special methods which Christ implemented to solve problems in people's lives.

In order to save ourselves from doom, it is necessary that we walk in the ways of the Lord and live according to His wisdom. God's ways are absolutely straight and sharp: He is unstoppable, because His judgment is perfect and true.

Generally, soldiers must not allow potential hindrances to damage their focus. Hindrances can be very dangerous, especially if they are not identified on time and dealt with effectively. However, it is better to do what is necessary to prevent the occurrence of hindrances before they become too difficult to overcome. It is important that soldiers seek to turn their weaknesses into strengths. In doing so, they learn to overcome their fears and turn their flaws into assets. Conversely, if recruits are lazy to begin with, their experience in the army will help them to get rid of that habit and become energetic and active. In addition, they learn to be confident and responsible individuals. Their weaknesses are turned into strengths. Likewise, when a new Christian does not know how to pray to counteract the powers of darkness, their spiritual education gives them the knowledge and power they need to become spiritually active. Through this, they become zealous believers.

Discipline is a fruit of the spirit which may yield positive results. It also creates a certain pattern of behaviour that can automatically bring an exceptional level of honour in to people's lives. In the pursuit of education, students are expected to pass their exams in order to graduate, but that mostly depends on the kind of discipline they exercise during their training. However, despite the kind of training that students may receive from their various schools, if they do not appropriately apply it, they often fail to live up to their potential.

This has been happening in the Christian faith for many centuries. Some believers fail to achieve what God has planned for them, because they do not utilise the training they receive from God. Discipline equips us with the fundamental tools for fruitful development.

As we follow the Lord's instructions and live by His ways, we will know how to rise above our challenges. In the New Testament, we can learn from the uncommon discipline and unique character of Jesus Christ. From the account of the scriptures in the New Testament, you will notice that the Lord's ways were without fault; He knew how to make all the best decisions. There was nothing that could have led Jesus astray; absolutely nothing prevented Him from doing what He came to do because He was perfectly regimented. This was because Jesus only did what the Father did.

> *"Then Jesus answered and said to them, 'Most assuredly, I say to you, the Son can do nothing of Himself, but what He sees the Father do; for whatever He does, the Son also does in like manner. For the Father loves the Son, and shows Him all things that He Himself does; and He will show Him greater works than these, that you may marvel.'"*
> [John 5:19-20]

This is how God expects Christians to be. Being disciplined in the Lord will solidify us like immovable rocks and unstoppable forces. Through it, we will know exactly what to do, where to go and how to implement things accordingly. When we are disciplined in the Lord, we will know exactly what time to do whatever it is we are supposed to do. Also, it will prevent us from compromising our faith in the Lord.

Chapter Two

Reliance On The Word

"But He answered and said, 'It is written, Man shall not live by bread alone, but by every word that proceeds from the mouth of God.'"

[Matthew 4:4]

Discipline Through The Word

In order to conquer and rise above the powers of darkness, you need to habitually abide in/study the Word of God. The Word of God can teach you all things and can empower you to be the best of the best in everything you do. This is because the Word of God is the epitome of godliness and wisdom; the Word contains knowledge that is beyond the universe. It is through the Word of God that you and I can reach the pinnacle of all pinnacles. It is through the Word of God that we can step into the very depths of God's inexplicable mysteries.

Nowadays, the world is polluted with so many clever philosophies that are diametrically in opposition to the principles of Christianity.

However, the ways of Jesus Christ surpass all other doctrines in the world, because it is the answer to all things. The best way to receive true wisdom is through the Word of the Lord. Without the Word, it will be impossible for anyone to comprehend the administration of God's power. It is through the Word that our souls can be enriched and enlightened to experience the original essence of life. [John 1:1-5]

"Till I come, give attention to reading, to exhortation, to doctrine."

[1 Timothy 4:13]

It is necessary to meditate on the Word day and night; it must be in your spirit and in your heart daily. It must be embedded in your mind and in your mouth at all times. The Word contains an unimaginable power that can transform anything in life whether spiritual or physical. In addition to reading the Word, it is important to practice its teachings consistently. No child of God is complete without the Word. The only way that Christians can be fruitful is to apply the principles of God's Word in every aspect of their lives. Many people have become successfully established because they educated themselves in the Word. If you are well grounded and solidified in the Word, phenomenal things will occur within you, so that you will become who you are destined to be. Some believers are failing to be who God created them to be, because they often get involved in petty quarrels and meaningless debates, and neglect the Word of God.

Ironically, these quarrels are sometimes actually about the Word of God. This attitude causes us to be ineffective in the Kingdom. We can only possess our destiny if we practise a Christ-like attitude and conduct ourselves appropriately. The attitude of Christ is the only way that we can be conquerors. God always wants the best for us, but there are certain ways of thinking and behaving we must enthusiastically exercise on a daily basis, in order to gain not just the good, but also the very best. [Proverbs 4: 20-22]

> "My foot has held fast to His steps; I have kept His way and not turned aside. I have not departed from the commandment of His lips; I have treasured the words of His mouth more than my necessary food."
> [Job 23:11-12]

Notice that the above focuses on the power and vitality of the Word. Job declared that he esteemed the Word of God more than his necessary food. As necessary as food is for the human body, it cannot replace what only the Word of God can do. [John 4:32-38] Job understood the clarity of the Word; through the Word, he overcame all his trials. [John 12:35-36] The Word of God can fulfil everything in your life since it will never return void. [Isaiah 55:11] It is important to understand how substantial the Word of God is, and why it is the foundation of the Christian faith.

The Word is irreplaceable; without it, it would be impossible to grow spiritually. If you fail to feed on the Word of God, your spiritual life will be malnourished indeed. Earthly food can become scarce; people can suffer famine and other types of disasters, but the Word of God never fails. In my experience, I have learned that wherever the Word of God is applied consistently, there is order, deliverance, liberty, growth, healing, peace, prosperity and power. Conversely, wherever the Word of God is scarce, confusion and contention dominate. In the beginning, the Earth was without form and void. But, when God spoke His perfect Word, darkness disappeared and everything came into being. [Genesis 1:1-31]

Wherever you go and whatever you do, it is important to acknowledge the importance of God's Word and apply it to your life daily. [Joshua 1:8] God has instructed us to meditate on His Word day and night - it enables us to remain strong. In addition, it restrains us from behaving loosely. It is very important to meditate on the Word of God which contains everything we need to be who God created us to be. Therefore, when you abide in the Word, God makes it clear which way to go and all your paths will be straight.

Jesus Christ trained the disciples and taught them the principles of the Word. Through that they gained the spiritual power they needed to overcome the powers of darkness. In addition, they were instructed by the Lord to go out and teach the world the Word - to give light and hope to the lost, so that they would also learn how to overcome the wiles of the enemy.

> *"Go therefore and make disciples of all the nations, baptising them in the name of the Father and of the Son and of the Holy Spirit, teaching them to observe all things that I have commanded you; and lo, I am with you always, even to the end of the age."*
> [Matthew 28:19-20]

As mentioned earlier, the disciples proclaimed the Word

to all nations, because it is through the Word that people receive salvation. As the Word is preached and people receive spiritual insight, they can be converted and baptised. After receiving the teachings of the Word, it is important that they diligently and faithfully continue in the commandments of God. Note that the Christian life begins with the Word, continues with the Word, and ends with the Word. You can only accomplish your Christian goals through the Word; without the ingredients of the Word, you are bound to fail. You can excel far more than you could ever envision if you let the Word of God be your source of guidance. Therefore, pick up your Bible and make a change today.

If we focus on the life of Jesus Christ, we will notice that He matured perfectly because He was, and is, and always will be the Word. [John 1:14]

Our Lord spent most of his childhood educating Himself according to the teachings of the Word and He became a teacher even by the tender age of twelve. [Luke 2:46-49] Moreover, Christ is the Word and His name is above every name and every principality. [Philippians 2:9] At the mention of His Name, every knee shall bow and every tongue will confess that He is Lord. At the mention of the name of Jesus, anything that is contrary to God cannot stand. When you know the Word and apply it, you will overcome the most hazardous trials and God will exalt you into a position that is far above your enemies. [Philippians 2:10-11] For example, in the Bible, we are told of a centurion who needed the healing of the Lord on behalf of his servant who became very sick - to the point of death. He believed in the Word and he trusted that his servant would bounce back to life through the Word of God. Therefore, he asked Jesus to declare the Word of healing out of His mouth and send it to his house on behalf of his servant. The Centurion's household overcame the power over sickness because they relied on the Word of the Lord. [Matthew 8:6-8]

The Word Is A Tool For Deliverance

When Eve shared the forbidden fruit with Adam, he should have denied himself and put the will of God first. As the man, he should have stood firm in the Lord by rebuking her and the serpent as an act of obedience to God. God gave Adam the wisdom and the power to make the right decisions as a man created in the image of God. Eve also, could have rebuked the serpent, but she did not. She could have consulted Adam first in order to check if what she heard was true. Perhaps, she could have asked God if what the serpent said about Him was true. This is why it is very important to be careful of the things we hear from the mouths of others, especially those who appear to be good friends. It is paramount to check if what we hear people say about other individuals is true before we react.

Questions?

> *Could it be that the love Adam had for Eve was too much for him to resist her temptation?*

> *Perhaps Adam tried to reject Eve's proposition to taste the forbidden fruit, but she persisted.*

> *Could it be that Eve had already become so much like the serpent and had turned into an expert of manipulation - even to the point that Adam could not deny her?*

Very often, our relationship with individuals who are very dear to us can prevent us from taking the necessary stand against ungodly decisions. In my experience, there have been many situations in which I failed to prove my loyalty to God. This is because during those times, I was not well rooted in the Word as I am now. I can recall many instances in my life where it seemed impossible to be faithful to the Lord, especially when I did not have enough time to gather my thoughts to make the right choices. By the awesome grace of God, I eventually learned to apply the Word of God effectively in situations that often tried to pull me away from God's presence. God is still using His Word to teach me to think like Him. In fact, writing this book has helped me to capture and appreciate some of the many mysteries of the Word. There are relatives, friends and colleagues who are so important to us that we do not even realise when we do ungodly things to please them. However, this book is a great opportunity to make a change.

> *"Then the king of Israel gathered the prophets together, about four hundred men, and said to them, 'Shall I go against Ramoth Gilead to fight, or shall I refrain?' So they said, 'Go up, for the Lord will deliver it into the hand of the king.'"*
>
> [1 Kings 22:6]

The scripture shows that king Ahab was in charge of over four hundred prophets who only spoke lies to please him. The king was preparing to overtake the land of his enemies, and he required information from his prophets. All the prophets who worked for the king convinced him to think that God was going to give him the power to conquer Ramoth Gilead. The prophets lied to Ahab as an act of their loyalty and to impress him. This could have been because they were well pampered by the king and were governed by the spirit of Jezebel.

> *"The messenger who had gone to summon Micaiah said to him, 'Look, the other prophets without exception are predicting success for the king. Let your word agree with theirs, and speak favourably.' But Micaiah said, 'As surely as the LORD lives, I can only tell him what the LORD tells me.' When he arrived, the king asked him, 'Micaiah, shall we go to war against Ramoth Gilead, or not?' 'Attack and be victorious,' he answered, 'or the LORD will give it into the king's hand."*
>
> [1 Kings 22:13-15]

The scripture shows us that the Prophet Micaiah was not

afraid to defy king Ahab and was willing to speak only according the voice of God. However, he was persuaded to do the opposite; when he came face to face with the king, he chose to prophesy falsely to king Ahab in order to please him.

The Lord is not the author of confusion, but He completely values honesty, wisdom and humility. It is important that we live according to God's guidance and forsake anything that could manipulate us into pleasing people to our own spiritual detriment. As a matter of fact, such behaviour can take us out of the will of God and can even cause us to become the enemies of God. When God becomes your enemy, there is absolutely no-one who can help you, unless you repent.

> *"And all the prophets prophesied so, saying, 'Go up to Ramoth Gilead and prosper, for the LORD will deliver it into the king's hand.'"*
>
> [1 Kings 22:12]

King Ahab's authority over his prophets did not allow them to speak the truth. In most cases, circumstances have caused multitudes of people to feel pressured to make decisions in order to please their peers. This is one of the several ways that curses have reigned in the lives of many and have destroyed multitudes of good people.

> *"The LORD said to him, 'In what way?' So he said, 'I will go out and be a lying spirit in the mouth of all his prophets.' And the LORD said, 'You shall persuade him, and also prevail. Go out and do so.' Therefore look! The LORD has put a lying spirit in the mouth of all these prophets of yours, and the LORD has declared disaster against you."*
>
> [1 Kings 22:22-23]

This passage in the Old Testament helps us to capture the fact that God put a lying spirit in the mouths of all the prophets of Ahab because they were not genuine seers of the Lord. God was aware that the prophets who often prophesied to king Ahab always spoke in compliance with Ahab's request and did not speak in accordance with the Spirit of the Lord. This passage also indicates that all the prophets who were under the authority of king Ahab were subject to the devil. Furthermore, this also comes as a great counsel to all those who are in Christ; it is of paramount importance to be careful of the people from whom we seek answers.

There are many genuine prophets today who are staunchly under the leadership of the Holy Ghost. However, there are multitudes of prophets in the world who are also under the influence of Satan, and who do not give counsel according to the ordinances of the Lord. Let us be reminded that such satanic prophets are subject to curses, because they are not accredited by the Holy Ghost. Therefore, be careful of who you permit to lay hands on you, and anoint you. Be careful of the kind of prophets you allow to influence you. God Himself can teach you the difference between a genuine and a false prophet, if you pray and ask Him for guidance. As for God, He will never leave you nor forsake you; He will never lie to or manipulate you, because He is a righteous God. He will always show you who is of the light and who is of the darkness.

> "Then Micaiah answered, 'I saw all Israel scattered on the hills like sheep without a shepherd, and the LORD said, These people have no master. Let each one go home in peace.'"
>
> [1 Kings 22:17]

Prophet Micaiah began to speak the truth and prophesied in correspondence with the Spirit of God. At this point, the prophet of God had become staunch and upright again not to be swayed by king Ahab or anyone else. Though all four hundred prophets spoke falsely in order to please the king, but Micaiah did not hesitate to stand for God regardless of what was going to happen to him. Though he spoke falsely in the beginning, this time he was not reluctant to reveal the oracles of God. Sometimes, we fail to do what God requires of us because of the fear of what the enemy could do to us. King Ahab did not allow Micaiah to get away with speaking the truth.

Very often, we hear of powerful men and women of God who come under great scrutiny and persecution as a result of their diligent service to God. It is often the wicked plans of the enemy that are devised against them to tarnish their image.

Prophet Micaiah was imprisoned and tortured because he chose to please God instead of man. The Devil is always waiting to attack us for speaking the truth and for doing what is right in the sight of the Lord. Nevertheless, it is more rewarding to do God's will-against all odds. [1 Kings 22:24-27]

It is crucial that Christians, especially prophets, speak only what comes out of the mouth of God and not verbally express what they think is right in the sight of man. It is critical to do the will of God in order to glorify God, and refrain from any falsehood which will exalt others or ourselves. Doing things in order to appear good in the eyes of people is a form of hypocrisy and idol worship. [Exodus 20:3] Anything we do which only glorifies something or someone else in place of God can take us on a path to destruction.

The aftermath of Adam and Eve's disobedience to the Lord was indeed regrettable because it brought multitudes of curses to the human race. Unfortunately, some of the curses will remain until the Lord returns. Those who refuse to give their lives to Christ and choose to do the will of the devil will be eternally doomed. It is important that we connect with people who have the fear of the Lord. It is crucial that we completely rely on the Word of God to cultivate our walk with the Lord, so that we will not compromise in doing what is right. Ungodly influences will only cause us to do what is contrary to God, but the godly will motivate us to do only what is pleasing to the Lord.

God gave Adam the Word which he should have used to

counteract Satan's lies. God would have surely exalted him and rebuked the devil, but Adam decided to disobey God's instructions, and this led mankind into sin. Adam had the authority to correct the situation, but he did not do so. In this case, Adam failed to be effective because he could not instruct Eve according to God's will; he did not stand on the principles which God gave him as a man, so he failed.

There are things that will threaten and attempt to destroy you. They may come in various shapes and sizes and from different directions, but it is the correct application of the Word that will protect you from all opposition. Just as God uses His Word to instruct us to do the right thing, Adam should have instructed Eve with the Word God gave him.

It is essential that we all learn from his pitiful mistake. It is our duty to sanctify the world with the Word by sharing it with others. It is very necessary to apply the Word of God to every situation in our lives in order to avoid destruction. Many great people have fallen short of the glory of God because they failed to make good use of the Word. When you fail to apply the teachings of the Word, you will miss out on its full power to help you become an overcomer.

Perhaps Eve would have been cleansed if Adam had applied the Word to exercise his authority as the head over her life. He could have saved them both and the entire human race if only he relied on the Word and resisted the temptation to sin against God.

Questions:

> *Who is in your life that you can "redeem" from evil?*
>
> *Who have you met lately that you can share the Word of God with?*

It could be a brother, or a sister who needs to be touched by the Holy Ghost. It could be a friend or a colleague at work. Perhaps it is a distant relative, or a total stranger you bump into. Christians often speak negatively of Adam for yielding to Eve, many of us often do the same as he did even though Christ has empowered us to be more than conquerors. [Romans 8:37]

This is an example of what can happen when you allow yourself to be distracted by things that are contrary to God. There are many things which often hinder Christians from applying the Word. Instead of taking the stand to resist, we prefer to sin first and think later. It is the knowledge and power of the Word that can enable us to overcome; so, do your best to read the Bible and live by it daily. [James 4:7]

Question:

Why do believers sometimes struggle to apply the Word as a tool of deliverance?

Ignorance and pride are two things that often prevent us from utilising the Word of God in every situation. Sometimes, we fail to apply the Word in order to deliver ourselves from evil situations, because we often perceive temptations as things we can 'throttle with our bare hands'.

This usually occurs when we rely on our human strength and our own understanding. [Acts 19:13-16] The Devil always brings suggestions that tantalise the desires of our flesh, so that our understanding will not be in line with God's Word. Such, was the trick he used on Adam and Eve, which persuaded them to disregard God's instructions in order to satisfy their flesh. They did not rely on God's instructions but allowed doubt to take over their minds. The doubt was placed in Eve's mind when the serpent, who is also the Devil [Revelation 12:8-9], caused her to question God's word as being untrustworthy, and Adam likewise. [Genesis 3:4-5] This is how the enemy has crept into the minds of many believers. Although we know that we cannot live without God, too often, we do not apply His principles, but allow suspicion to sneak into our minds and cause us to lose our trust in Him.

One of the most ridiculous ideas I have heard is the belief that our guardian angels will do all the hard work, so providing ourselves an excuse to shirk our responsibility to guard ourselves against temptation. Although Angels are assigned to assist us in so many ways, it is better to be soaked in the Word of God, which is full of power. After all, angels are also creatures and not the Creator. It is plausible that angels were also spoken into existence by the Word of God. [Psalm 33:6] Many Christians believe that they are safe from circumstances just because they are in Christ, and so they neglect to educate themselves with the Word of God as they should.

Being a Christian does not exempt you from being caught up in storms. Being a child of God does not make you immune to temptation and affliction. But if you know the Word of God and saturate yourself in it daily, your safety and survival will be assured.

The Power In The Word

> *"So shall My word be that goes forth from My mouth; It shall not return to Me void, but it shall accomplish what I please, And it shall prosper in the thing for which I sent it."*
>
> [Isaiah 55:11]

We battle against invisible forces daily, but the Word of the Lord contains the kind of power that is more than able to control and destroy them all. Also, the Word is Spirit and life and there is nothing that can stand in its path. [John 6:63] This scripture reminds us that God's Word is a formidable power which and always prevails, because:

> *"In the beginning was the Word, and the Word was with God, and the Word was God."*
>
> [John 1:1]

The Bible is powerful since, as well as being the Word, it is a written representation of God's character. It is His thoughts, His feelings, His actions and the significance of His existence. The Word has the power to heal [Matthew 20], the muscle to cast out demons [Mark 5], to liberate us from demonic oppression [Luke 8], the potency to destroy evil [Isaiah 34], the power to resurrect [John 11], and the authority to bring restoration as it did in the valley of the dry bones. [Ezekiel 37]

God's Word is the epitome of unlimited power; it has the capacity to curse and destroy. It is also important to be careful about what comes out of your mouth. It is important to hold your tongue as much as possible until you are very sure that what you intend to say will be profitable to yourself and others.

The words that come out of our mouths can either edify or destroy ourselves or others. Misuse of God's Word can open doors of circumstances against us. We will be held accountable for every word that comes out of our mouth, even careless words. [Matthew 12:36] This is not to say that the Word is like some occultic incantation, but as James observes *"You ask and do not receive, because you ask amiss, that you may spend it on your pleasures."* [James 4:3]

There is nothing that can stand in the way of God's Word, because it is the light that conquers all darkness. [John 1:5] The Word of God never disappoints; it is perfect and true. There is nothing and no-one in the entire universe who can escape the presence of God [Isaiah 55:11] and He will release His Word according to His sovereign will and purposes. [Isaiah 55:8-9]

Questions:

Can God ever come back to tell you that He failed to conquer your enemies?

Can God ever say that He could not find what you lost?

Can the Lord ever return to you and complain that He fell asleep on the way and missed His timing?

Can God ever come back to tell you that the enemy was too much for Him to deal with?

Can God ever come back to you and tell you that the curse that has been afflicting your family for generations was too much for Him to break?

Can God ever open His mouth and say that He did not have enough support to destroy that stronghold that stood in your way?

Can the One whose height cannot be measured ever come back to tell you that the evil giant in your life was too tall for Him?

Can the One whose wonders are immeasurable ever come back to tell us that He has grown weary and cannot carry on anymore?

Think about this for a moment.

The Word is 'the sword of the Spirit,' it is the most formidable weapon that exists. [Ephesians 6:17] The Bible also tells us that, the Word is *"sharper than any two-edged sword"* because it has the power to cut through anything even the things that an ordinary two-edged sword cannot penetrate. [Hebrews 4:12] One side of the Sword–the Word, contains the judgment of God, and the other side represents the merciful side of God. However, both sides of the Word are impeccably effective. On the other hand, *"the two-edged"* sword is also a reflection of the Old Testament and the New Testament which are both absolute. The Old Testament mostly revealed the strict side of God, but the New Testament showed us the complete love of the Lord for us through the death of Christ on the Cross. Nevertheless, both Old and New Testament form the complete Word, which reflect the mind and character of God.

> *"I have come as a light into the world, that whoever believes in Me should not abide in darkness."*
> [John 12:46]

The Word of God is light: it enables us to see where we are

going. [Psalm 119:105] When the Word is in operation, it exposes all the things that can potentially harm us along the way. [2 Corinthians 4:4-6] This means that the Word illuminates the path at our feet and it shows us what we need for the moment. [Psalm 119:105] It can give you supernatural perception. In other words, the Word of God can guide and protect us from falling into any spiritual potholes and any hidden traps that our enemies have set up for us. Imagine yourself in the middle of the night, especially in an environment that has no lights; it is obvious that most people are likely to experience an amount of fear in such a place because it is difficult to identify danger in darkness.

This is why marauders usually operate at night because darkness gives them the cover they need. This makes it easier for them to attack their victims. The world is covered in darkness because it is overwhelmed with evil, but it is the Word of God that enables all believers to see what the devil and his demons are plottiing against us. This is why we always gain hope when we have insight into what is ahead of us. In addition to hope, light also brings joy, peace, confidence and celebration.

Many festivals often use fireworks to begin or end their celebrations: fireworks light up the skies at night. This causes people to cheer and shout for joy; such is the effect of the Word. That is why Christ came to die for the world, because He is the light of the world. [John 8:12] Without the light of Christ to shine upon the world, darkness will reign. Without the Word of God in you, darkness will govern your life. [John 3:17-21]

> *"All Scripture is given by inspiration of God, and is profitable for doctrine, for reproof, for correction, for instruction in righteousness."*
> [2 Timothy 3:16]

The Word brings liberty to those who believe in it. Therefore, as you live by the Word, it will undoubtedly set you free. [John

8:32] The Word also brings correction, because it has a duty to overcome evil or to turn it into good. Without the Word of God to guide us, life would be unfruitful indeed. We cannot be true disciples of Christ if we fail to apply the Word of God in our lives. [John 8:31] Therefore, we must do our very best to saturate ourselves with the Word daily and with enthusiasm, so that we will exhibit the fruits of the Spirit - love, joy, peace, long-suffering, kindness, goodness, faithfulness, gentleness and self-control. [Galatians 5:22-23]

Chapter Three

Obedience And Disobedience

> *"Now the word of the LORD came to Jonah the son of Amittai, saying, 'Arise, go to Nineveh, that great city, and cry out against it; for their wickedness has come up before Me.' But Jonah arose to flee to Tarshish from the presence of the LORD. He went down to Joppa, and found a ship going to Tarshish; so he paid the fare, and went down into it, to go with them to Tarshish from the presence of the LORD."*
>
> [Jonah 1: 1-3]

Servant Of Rebellion

The prophet Jonah experienced the chastisement of God because he refused to comply with God's instruction, but God did not destroy him. God, in His mercy, spared Jonah's life so that he would have the opportunity to repent. Notice in the Bible passage above that Jonah refused to obey the Lord; rather, he tried to remove himself from God's presence. This also means that Jonah knew God's voice; he knew it was God who spoke to him, because he was close to God - yet, he chose to rebel.

Jonah chose to behave like a headstrong goat instead of humbling himself like a sheep. The great prophet of God allowed his distorted values to dominate his relationship with the Lord. Although we may have spent time getting to know God, we still choose to disobey Him like stubborn goats. This occurs because many Christians are still living according to the carnal mind and will do so until Christ comes and completes that which He has started in us. [Philippians 1:6] Sometimes, we do not respond to the voice of the Lord, especially when we allow too many contrary things to overshadow our understanding. When you allow certain things to block your senses, it can affect your relationship with God. Sometimes, God instructs us to go in a particular direction to accomplish certain things, but we often choose to move in the direction that only leads us into chaos. There are times when we think we know better than God and do what we feel is best.

> *"But the* LORD *sent out a great wind on the sea, and there was a mighty tempest on the sea, so that the ship was about to be broken up. Then the mariners were afraid; and every man cried out to his god, and threw the cargo that was in the ship into the sea, to lighten the load. But Jonah had gone down into the lowest parts of the ship, had lain down, and was fast asleep."*
>
> [Jonah 1:4-5]

Note the verse *"and cried every man unto his god..."* This indicates that there were people on the ship who worshipped other gods. This is what can happen when you remove yourself from the presence of God - you can end up in the midst of those who do not worship the same God as you do. Some leave the Kingdom and go back into the world - into nightclubs, bars, strip joints, casinos and similar. These are all places where other gods rule. There are also activities and events that can pull us away from the Kingdom. Many ungodly television shows and films have the potential to lead us away from God and into the mouth of darkness. Therefore, it is important to remember that when you remove yourself from God's supervision, you take away the umbrella that He has placed over you.

Moreover, you remove the blessings and the anointing that He has placed on your life–including many benefits such as healing, joy and peace. Your absence from God can invite ungodly spirits into your life. Such is the damaging effect of a tempest - it can remove every comfort we have and bring an enormous amount of confusion, pain, sorrow and death into our lives. This is why we must always remain in God's presence and obey His instruction so that we will be safe from disaster.

Curse By Association

> *"So the captain came to him, and said to him, 'What do you mean, sleeper? Arise, call on your God; perhaps your God will consider us, so that we may not perish.' And they said to one another, 'Come, let us cast lots, that we may know for whose cause this trouble has come upon us.' So they cast lots, and the lot fell on Jonah."*
>
> [Jonah 1:6-7]

Although Jonah was God's servant, he brought a curse upon the men on the ship. Before he embarked, the men were travelling in peace and had expectations of a good journey. However, Jonah's presence brought a lot of confusion. As the mariners cast their lots, they discovered the culprit. Sometimes, you have to cast away certain things in order to discover the reason behind all the calamities that are going on in your life. The mariners cast their lots - *"So they cast lots, and the lot fell upon Jonah."* This is to signify that when you rebel against God, the consequences that others around you experience as a result of your sin will eventually fall upon you. When David sinned against God, he incurred severe penalties on the people as well as himself. [2 Samuel 24:1-17]

The lots the mariners cast may represent the baggage that people carry in their lives. This means that as their lots fell upon Jonah, sometimes the baggage of others will fall upon you, especially if you are not meant to be in their midst. The baggage of others could be curses, demonic oppression, incurable diseases and so forth. Jonah was not meant to be on that ship, because he was meant to be in the city of Nineveh. Confusion and disaster can overwhelm us when we take ourselves into places we are not supposed to be.

Notice that the verse says Jonah was asleep while the mariners struggled to stay alive. Very often, our eyes are closed to the troubles we bring to other people, especially when we are too conceited to realise our faults. When your eyes are closed, you will not see the repercussions that are about to fall upon you. When you are blind, you will fail to see the chaos that surrounds you. When you are spiritually unaware, you will not often recognize the damage that can occur in your life and in the lives of others around you. This is another demonstration regarding those who sin and let all the consequences fall upon innocent people whilst they continue–oblivious to the damage. Often people are ignorant of the troubles that follow them into the lives of other people; this is one of the reasons why it is important to examine ourselves daily and humbly come to terms with our errors. Whilst others work extra hard to progress, there are some who just enjoy their comforts at the expense of others.

The mariners suffered because of Jonah's disobedience yet when Jonah boarded the ship, they could not have imagined that such a disaster was about to overwhelm them. There are times that you may find yourself surrounded by trouble and wonder where it came from and how it found a foothold into your life. This is usually the result of the people we associate with.

Therefore, it is important to be wise concerning the friends we keep and the activities they are involved in. This does not mean that you must deliberately look for somebody to blame for the disasters that occur in your life, because the perpetrator could be you. Examine yourself and ask if you are being disobedient to God. There are times that you might not even know it, but you have the opportunity to discover if you have been ignoring that still small voice. We will constantly experience very serious setbacks in our lives if we continue to neglect God. Jonah fell into despair because the presence of God was an imposition to him.

Personal Examination

Question:

Why was the presence of God such a nuisance to Jonah?

There are times that believers treat God as if He is a hindrance, but not all of us are aware of that. Sometimes, we are too proud and stubborn to listen when God speaks to us. Very often, it is easy for us to forget about God when we become successful. King Saul became so wrapped up with fame and glory that he thought he could do things his own way. When he was supposed to pay attention to God and do His will, he focused on the attention he received from his people. [1 Samuel 15]

There are believers today who are going astray from God's presence in order to be comfortable and choose their own way of life. It is God who created us and not the other way round; therefore, it is imperative that we decrease self-glory as much as possible and allow our reverence for God's Sovereignty to increase each day.

It is crucial to remember that God is everywhere; He sees everything we do and knows everywhere we go. He hears everything we say and can read every thought in our minds, because He is omnipotent and omniscient. Consequently, even if we run to the ends of the earth, we cannot escape from God. [Psalm 139:1-12] We should know that God is always good and He only wants the best for us. It is important to acknowledge Him daily.

> "Then they said to him, 'Please tell us! For whose cause is this trouble upon us? What is your occupation? And where do you come from? What is your country? And of what people are you?' So he said to them, 'I am a Hebrew; and I fear the LORD, the God of heaven, who made the sea and the dry land.'"
>
> [Jonah 1:8-9]

Even as children of God, there are things we do that cause unbelievers to question us. Jonah had already told the mariners who he was, so their further questioning suggests he had done something wrong. There are times that I myself question our behaviour as believers of Christ.

Perhaps, havoc has taken over your life because you started a career in the wrong place. Maybe, things are falling on top of you because you have established a ministry without God's approval. It is possible that you have been seeking counsel from the wrong people. Nevertheless, you have the opportunity to repent, so that God will lead you back to your Nineveh. Children of God are supposed to be exceptional examples to the world; God wants us to be beacons of hope, so that we can lead unbelievers to Christ.

> *"Then they said to him, 'What shall we do to you that the sea may be calm for us?'- for the sea was growing more tempestuous. And he said to them, 'Pick me up and throw me into the sea; then the sea will become calm for you. For I know that this great tempest is because of me.' Nevertheless the men rowed hard to return to land, but they could not, for the sea continued to grow more tempestuous against them. Therefore they cried out to the LORD and said, 'We pray, O LORD, please do not let us perish for this man's life, and do not charge us with innocent blood; for You, O LORD, have done as it pleased You.'"*
>
> [Jonah 1:11-14]

Just as the people on the ship began to understand, it is important for us to also appreciate that the best thing to do is to surrender to God. The mariners came to acknowledge the awesome power of God. As the Bible passage declares, the mariners on the ship became exceedingly afraid as they witnessed the greatness of the tempest. Because of what the fishermen saw and what they experienced, they began to set the example that Jonah failed to implement. This strongly proves that there are unbelievers who can recognize the awesomeness of God and show Him reverence even more than Christians.

In other words, God accomplished His own mission through the storm and through the people on the ship, because of Jonah's refusal to go and prophesy to Nineveh. We are servants of the Lord and God is the original and ultimate

King who is Sovereign in all His ways. Therefore, it is wise to comply with whatever God instructs us to do regardless of what we think or how we feel. There is no one who can deny the supernatural power of the Almighty God; He is our Creator and Master.

> *"So they picked up Jonah and threw him into the sea, and the sea ceased from its raging. Then the men feared the LORD exceedingly, and offered a sacrifice to the LORD and took vows."*
>
> [Jonah 1:15-16]

It was a successful outcome for the people on the ship because they all came to acknowledge the supremacy of God. The most important thing about this story is that the mariners made a sacrifice to God, and then they made vows. This suggests that a conversion may have taken place. The people had come to a point in which they surrendered their lives to the one true God. It is important to recognize that there is no other power greater than the Omnipotent God.

The Indignation And The Mercy Of The Lord

> *"Now the LORD had prepared a great fish to swallow Jonah. And Jonah was in the belly of the fish three days and three nights."*
>
> [Jonah 1:17]

Considering the calamity that Jonah caused, God still exercised mercy upon him and he was still alive in the belly of the great fish for the duration of three days. The fish did not digest him; the bones in the fish did not crush him and the muscles in the belly of the fish did not suffocate him. Jonah could have died on the ship during the great tempest, but he did not. He could have drowned in the sea when the mariners threw him overboard, but he did not die because God protected him. It is by the mercy of God that we are all alive today. God's faithfulness, kindness, grace and His unfailing love continues to sustain us daily. Therefore, it is critical that we continuously recognise God and reverence Him for all the wonderful things He does in our lives. God is our great Redeemer.

> "Then Jonah prayed to the LORD his God from the fish's belly. And he said: 'I cried out to the LORD because of my affliction, And He answered me. Out of the belly of Sheol I cried, and You heard my voice. For You cast me into the deep, Into the heart of the seas, and the floods surrounded me; all Your billows and Your waves passed over me. Then I said, I have been cast out of Your sight; Yet I will look again toward Your holy temple.'"
>
> [Jonah 2:1-4]

Jonah realised that he was in a situation that was totally beyond his control; he did not have the power to save himself, so he had to repent. Whilst he was in the belly of the great fish, God heard his prayer and forgave him. This is something to learn from; it is better to humble ourselves and take every opportunity to repent from our sins so that God will have mercy upon us. It is wise and fruitful to obey the Lord and always trust in Him. Without God, we are nothing.

> "Now the word of the LORD came to Jonah the second time, saying, 'Arise, go to Nineveh, that great city, and preach to it the message that I tell you.'
>
> So Jonah arose and went to Nineveh, according to the word of the LORD. Now Nineveh was an exceedingly great city, a three-day journey in extent. And Jonah began to enter the city on the first day's walk. Then he cried out and said, 'Yet forty days, and Nineveh shall be overthrown!'
>
> So the people of Nineveh believed God, proclaimed a fast, and put on sackcloth, from the greatest to the least of them. Then word came to the king of Nineveh; and he arose from his throne and laid aside his robe, covered himself with sackcloth and sat in ashes."
>
> [Jonah 3:1-6]

Now, we see that Jonah changed his ways as a result of his experience with the Tempest and the time he spent in the belly of the great fish. He could not have imagined that the people of Nineveh would turn from their evil ways. However, God already knew that the city of Nineveh was prepared to do the will of God provided they were alerted to their wrongdoings. Furthermore, this remarkable passage should help us to understand that it is not up to us to judge who we think will do the will of God and who will not. It is only God who knows the heart of every human being on earth. It is only God who knows who will repent and do His will and who will disobey Him. It is necessary that we ask God to give us the courage to go exactly where He instructs us to go.

> *"And he caused it to be proclaimed and published throughout Nineveh by the decree of the king and his nobles, saying, Let neither man nor beast, herd nor flock, taste anything; do not let them eat, or drink water. But let man and beast be covered with sackcloth, and cry mightily to God; yes, let every one turn from his evil way and from the violence that is in his hands. Who can tell if God will turn and relent, and turn away from His fierce anger, so that we may not perish? Then God saw their works, that they turned from their evil way; and God relented from the disaster that He had said He would bring upon them, and He did not do it."*
>
> [Jonah 3:7-10]

Questions:

Now, can we imagine the lives we could save if we comply with God's instructions daily?

Can we now understand the impact we could make in our lives as well as the lives of other people?

We can clearly see from the Bible passage that through Jonah's obedience a major city was saved from destruction.

Because Jonah repented and learned to comply with God's instructions, he became a deliverer. God wants to use us to do the same, so that many will turn their hearts away from the ways of the devil and receive the salvation of Christ. God can use us to save many nations if only we surrender to Him.

As much as Jonah was a *'bona fide'* prophet, there were certain characteristics in him which displeased God; therefore, it was necessary for him to experience disciplinary action in order to induce him to change his ways.

Perhaps, confusion has taken over your life because you have become the 'Jonah' to your family and friends. Possibly, you have turned against your congregation because you do not want to accept the necessary changes. Perchance, you have become a 'Jonah' to your own spouse by paying more attention to individuals, or issues that could destroy your marriage. It could be that you have become unemployed because you chose to behave like 'Jonah' towards your boss. When you think you know better than God, it will be very easy to fall into misery.

It is essential to acknowledge that God has never been wrong and He will never ever be wrong in anything because He is sovereign and omniscient. Rather, we are the ones who are often wrong because we are imperfect; that is why we are under God's training daily. Therefore, it is necessary to humble ourselves and remain in the presence of the Lord all the days of our lives. When we are not in God's presence, many things can destroy us.

Nineveh is a type, a symbol, of 'the world and the unbelievers.' Conversely, Jonah, the man of God, symbolises the Church. There are those who have the gift to reach out to the lost souls in the world. However, it is essential that those whom God assigns to minister to the unsaved, act as they are instructed. It was necessary for Jonah to be humbled through his experience with the great storm before he could go to Nineveh and bring about a mighty change. God already knew that Jonah would disobey Him and that the great storm would be the best method of chastisement, to bring about transformation. Sometimes, believers must go through a special kind of preparation in order to bring an effectual change in the world. That special preparation can be seen in many ways. Certain storms are compulsory because God allows them to manifest as a process of admonishment to strengthen and straighten out His people.

It was obvious that Jonah's attitude towards God and his responsibilities changed after the experience of the storm. Likewise, when Christians go through some persecutions and trials, it could be that God is about to cause a special change. Sometimes, the storms you face are God's indignation upon you to help you to become a better person, so that He can use you effectively.

Strengths And Weaknesses

Question:

What are some of the things that create weaknesses in the Church?

It may be that many members in your congregation are oblivious to God's calling upon their lives or that the members in your church are too slothful. It may be that your place of worship is too small and you want God to give you a bigger place to fellowship in; or, it could be that the flaws in your congregation have caused too many members to leave. It may be that most of the members of your congregation are not as unified and loving as they should be; or that there is severe lack of attendance. Sometimes, it could be lack of financial strength to uphold the functions of the church.

All these examples are some of the reasons why God allows the Church to experience some disruptions as a way of eradicating any activity that has the potential to undermine the progress of the Kingdom of God. In addition, the attitude of believers who mimic the behaviour of unbelievers around them can also cause problems in the Church.

Congregations also become weak because of the distorted values they hear and learn from those who teach them. Some believers fail to understand that Christianity is about following Jesus Christ and serving God and not about pleasing people.

In my experience, I have noticed that some believers are so afraid of losing the worldly respect they receive from others; thus, their thoughts and actions become a stronghold and a headache to the church. Sometimes, we are too comfortably set in our ways; often too impatient and unwilling to persevere according to God's guidance. [Ezekiel 36:25-28] These symptoms of carnality have caused serious deficits in the body of Christ, especially as there are many believers who are absenting themselves from their divine posts as a result of selfishness, pride and lack of understanding.

Soldiers do not leave their posts until they are properly relieved and initiated elsewhere; therefore, as a spiritual soldier of Christ, it is imperative to stay on course and in your rightful place with the assurance of the Lord and with boldness, dignity and determination until God instructs you otherwise. Your rightful post is being in the presence of the Lord. Being absent from your duties and walking in the opposite direction is an act of disobedience and disloyalty to God. Leaving the post where God has placed you could open the door to unimaginable consequences into your life.

When I was in secondary school, a number of the young students who were in the same class as me failed their exams because, instead of attending classes, they chose to engage in their own rebellious activities.

Whilst growing up, there were occasions when it seemed normal to be rebellious, but this resulted in severe consequences and some near-death situations. It is the grace of God that has brought me this far. This is an indication of what can happen when believers do not apply the principles of Christ in their lives.

The Kingdom of God is our academy or place of study, and Jesus Christ our Lord is the headmaster. Pastors are employed by God to educate us with the Word of God. Furthermore, if we continue to turn our backs on the very principles that have the potential to nurture and guarantee exceptional growth and establishment in our areas of calling, then we will surely fail regardless of how hard we try. As we humble ourselves in the presence of the Lord our God and trust Him, our lives will begin to change for the better. [Romans 8:28] Our willingness to change will help us all to complete our journey in Christ and will surely take us into the Promised Land - our eternal home.

The Power Of Obedience

> *"So I prophesied as I was commanded; and as I prophesied, there was a noise, and suddenly a rattling; and the bones came together, bone to bone. Indeed, as I looked, the sinews and the flesh came upon them, and the skin covered them over; but there was no breath in them. Also He said to me, 'Prophesy to the breath, prophesy, son of man, and say to the breath, Thus says the LORD God: Come from the four winds, O breath, and breathe on these slain, that they may live.' So I prophesied as He commanded me, and breath came into them, and they lived, and stood upon their feet, an exceedingly great army."*
>
> [Ezekiel 37:7-10]

The prophet Ezekiel was a unique servant of the Lord; he was a greatly-anointed man of God who was formidable in following divine instructions. God used him in a remarkable way because he was not reluctant to obey God's voice. When you totally surrender yourself to God, wonderful things can happen. We can also see the importance of faith without which we limit what God can do in our lives. Ezekiel had so much faith in God that he spoke the word of God as he was instructed. He did not waver, he did not think twice, but he fully trusted God and complied with His instructions.

As I read the Bible passage about the miracle in the valley of the dry bones, I realised that the prophet became a very powerful instrument for God [Ezekiel 37:1]. Whilst this was a vision, it was a prophecy of what God will do at some time in the future, a resurrection of Israel physically to the Promised Land. When you allow God to use you as His vessel, a mighty restoration can occur.

There are situations in our lives that represent the dry bones in the valley. There are circumstances such as unfulfilled dreams, strongholds, limitations, infertility, unemployment, failed marriages and family breakdowns. Many believers are trying so hard, in their flesh to accomplish things, but they forget that they can only achieve God's plan for their lives when they are submitted to Him. Complying with God's instructions will definitely ensure that God's plan for your life becomes a reality, just like the dry bones in the valley. God's power is the master key that can open every door. Your obedience to God is what will qualify you to be an object of God's favour. Your obedience is a bridge to the glory of the Lord, but disobedience is like a house without a roof, because it will prevent you from being under God's covering.

> *"And they lived, and stood upon their feet, an exceedingly great army."*
>
> [Ezekiel 37:10]

The dry bones in the valley became an excessively fearful army. This account confirms that by the power of the Holy Spirit, every dead situation can, if God commands be resurrected, to become even greater than before and no one will be able to stand against you. As long as you rely on God's power, He will enable you to do what you cannot do in your own strength. God can use you more effectively and take you deeper, further and higher than you can ever imagine but only if you obey Him.

The Power Of God's Presence

> "And the LORD said to Moses, 'Cut two tablets of stone like the first ones, and I will write on these tablets the words that were on the first tablets which you broke. So be ready in the morning, and come up in the morning to Mount Sinai, and present yourself to Me there on the top of the mountain. And no man shall come up with you, and let no man be seen throughout all the mountain; let neither flocks nor herds feed before that mountain.' So he cut two tablets of stone like the first ones. Then Moses rose early in the morning and went up Mount Sinai, as the LORD had commanded him; and he took in his hand the two tablets of stone."
>
> [Exodus 34:1-4]

This Bible passage reveals how much Moses prioritised his relationship with God. It was certainly arduous to lead the children of Israel out of Egypt and through the wilderness. As gruelling as it was at his age to ascend Mount Sinai in the early hours of the morning, Moses did not hesitate to do what God instructed him to do. Moses could have used so many excuses to avoid the task, but he complied without any sign of complaint or rebellion. There are Christians today for whom it is difficult to take a single step for God, because of their pride and their worldly values. Moses' attitude towards the Lord was what made him a remarkable servant in the Kingdom and his name remains one of the most unforgettable in the entire human race. Your obedience to God can turn you into a spiritual giant.

> "Then the LORD said to Moses: 'Write these words, for according to the tenor of these words I have made a covenant with you and with Israel.'"
>
> [Exodus 34:27]

God made a covenant with Moses and all Israel because of

Moses' desire to do God's will. Moses is undoubtedly one of the most exceptional role-models in the Bible because of his immense contribution to the Kingdom. The obedience of one person can save a whole generation. It was through Noah's obedience that his family survived the great flood. It was through Isaac's obedience that he reaped a hundredfold and became great. It was Abraham's obedience to God that qualified him to be the father of many nations. It was the obedience of Jesus Christ that brought Salvation to the world.

It is imperative to remind ourselves of those whose legacies have helped to establish Christianity on Earth in a remarkable fashion. It is wise to follow in the footsteps of wonderful characters such as Elijah, Elisha, David, Tabitha, Ruth, Mary Magdalene and the prolific Apostle Paul, as well as many others who sacrificed and helped to pave the way for us. Notwithstanding, you too have the opportunity today to do the will of God, so that He will make your name great.

Questions:

What will your story be?

How will you be remembered?

Will your life be a great inspiration to others and the world?

Will you make a difference to mankind?

Will your life be a significant commemoration like our teachers in the Bible?

If you abide in God and obey Him, He will surely add your name to the history books. As our Christian journey continues and as we walk in the footsteps of great men and women who had gone before us, we will surely experience the wonderful works of the Lord.

The Glory Of The Lord

> *"Now it was so, when Moses came down from Mount Sinai (and the two tablets of the Testimony were in Moses' hand when he came down from the mountain), that Moses did not know that the skin of his face shone while he talked with Him. So when Aaron and all the children of Israel saw Moses, behold, the skin of his face shone, and they were afraid to come near him. Then Moses called to them, and Aaron and all the rulers of the congregation returned to him; and Moses talked with them. Afterward all the children of Israel came near, and he gave them as commandments all that the LORD had spoken with him on Mount Sinai. And when Moses had finished speaking with them, he put a veil on his face."*
>
> [Exodus 34:29-33]

When God appeared to Moses on the mountain of Sinai as he waited on the Lord for forty days and forty nights, his face was transfigured and shone like the sun. This Bible passage revealed how important it is to spend quality time with God. The presence of the Lord is Holy and contains healing, love, strength and everything that defies the laws of darkness. If you enjoy the presence of God daily, your life will never be the same. This means that as you stay close to God and obey Him, you will become like Him.

> *"But if the ministry of death, written and engraved on stones, was glorious, so that the children of Israel could not look steadily at the face of Moses because of the glory of his countenance, which glory was passing away."*
>
> [2 Corinthians 3:7]

It is evident that God reflected Himself through Moses because He wanted the children of Israel to experience Him. If God revealed Himself in totality to anyone, that creature would die, so He showed Himself through Moses instead.

> *"But He said, 'You cannot see My face; for no man shall*

> *see Me, and live.'"*
>
> [Exodus 33:20]

As the children of Israel saw Moses' luminous face, it gave them a very faint idea of what God looks like. This must have helped the children of Israel to reverence God more. As the Jewish people in the New Testament experienced the image of the Father through Jesus Christ, the children of Israel also experienced God through Moses [John 14:9-11]

God's presence can do things that no human being on Earth can ever imagine. Moses was a very old man at that time; but because of his time with God, his physical appearance became a phenomenon. You can be young or old, weak or strong; but when God's presence overwhelms you, your life will experience vibrancy, power and glory.

Indeed, as new creations of God, we too are being transformed daily into the likeness of Christ. As Paul says - *"... for now we see in a mirror dimly, but then face to face. Now I know in part, but then I shall know just as I also am known."* [1 Corinthians 13:12] One day, we shall see the glory that God now sees in us through Jesus Christ.

Chapter Four

The Effects Of The Past

> *"Brethren, I do not count myself to have apprehended; but one thing I do, forgetting those things which are behind and reaching forward to those things which are ahead, I press toward the goal for the prize of the upward call of God in Christ Jesus."*
>
> [Philippians 3:13-14]

The Past Is A Great Teacher

There are certain values that are necessary to acquire and there are some that are essential to avoid. Moreover, there are some things that must be completely relinquished from our lives. There are many flaws in the life of every individual, but the most important thing is to identify our strong and weak points in order to guide ourselves properly.

Question:

> *What are some of the things that will be profitable for you to avoid and what are those that are necessary for you to acquire?*

In life, one of the numerous things that must be avoided is the negative influence of the past. Many people are holding on to memories that continue to keep them trapped. This is what often happens when we are unable to let go of issues that are supposed to be behind us.

The past issues can become strongholds when we allow them to linger and ensnare us. This is something that prevents many people from making the necessary progress in their lives. When we dwell too much on the past, it can cause us to procrastinate; and if we continue to postpone, we become inactive. The past is like dust under a carpet, which some clean up before they lay a new carpet whilst others leave it. They forget that one day the carpet will need replacing. In doing so, that dirt they left behind will still be there and stuck to both the floor and the carpet.

When the time comes to lay a new carpet, that dirt will be very difficult to get rid of, because it would have become ingrained over a very long time.

There are errors from the past that continue to affect us in one way or another, because they were left unattended for so long. When we make up our minds to eradicate them, it will not be so easy to erase them. It is imperative that we know how to leave the past behind.

When people die, those who mourn them may from time to time visit their grave, or marker if cremated, to remind them of the people they once knew. However, no one remains in a cemetery because it is only a place for the dead. Likewise, the past should be buried in the right place. You can visit it from time to time for reference, but you must not stay there. You can use your past mistakes and failures to shape your present and your future, but let the past remain where it is regardless of how substantial it was.

There are some things that may come back to 'haunt' us if we refuse to let them go. That is why we may have to bury some things in case they manifest themselves again. Nevertheless, it is important to distinguish between what needs to be buried and what needs to be totally eradicated from our lives. The past can be good or bad, it depends on how we perceive it; it may also contain the blueprints to the future. This is because it possesses the necessary ideas that help to build our destiny. The past can teach us the difference between right and wrong; it can give us the wisdom and the knowledge to make our tomorrows better.

A good example was in the account of the rich man and the beggar named Lazarus. Let us go a little deeper to gain some understanding of how the past can teach us and show us the right way.

> *"There was a certain rich man who was clothed in purple and fine linen and fared sumptuously every day. But there*

> was a certain beggar named Lazarus, full of sores, who was laid at his gate, desiring to be fed with the crumbs which fell from the rich man's table. Moreover the dogs came and licked his sores.
>
> So it was that the beggar died, and was carried by the angels to Abraham's bosom. The rich man also died and was buried. And being in torments in Hades, he lifted up his eyes and saw Abraham afar off, and Lazarus in his bosom. Then he cried and said, 'Father Abraham, have mercy on me, and send Lazarus that he may dip the tip of his finger in water and cool my tongue; for I am tormented in this flame.'
>
> But Abraham said, 'Son, remember that in your lifetime you received your good things, and likewise Lazarus evil things; but now he is comforted and you are tormented. And besides all this, between us and you there is a great gulf fixed, so that those who want to pass from here to you cannot, nor can those from there pass to us.'
>
> Then he said, 'I beg you therefore, father, that you would send him to my father's house, for I have five brothers, that he may testify to them, lest they also come to this place of torment.' Abraham said to him, 'They have Moses and the prophets; let them hear them.' And he said, 'No, father Abraham; but if one goes to them from the dead, they will repent.' But he said to him, 'If they do not hear Moses and the prophets, neither will they be persuaded though one rise from the dead.'"
>
> [Luke 16:19-31]

In this story, we see that it was too late for the rich man to sort things out; he was not going to get another chance to rectify his past. Although he regretted his mistakes, he could not come back to life to put things right.

One reason God allowed this story to be recorded is as a point of correction to teach us how to make the right choices whilst we are still alive. There are times that we fail to acknowledge the wrong we have done until an issue of the past comes back to confront us. In doing so, we can get the right understanding and the chance to make amends before we move on. It is evident that we will certainly not have the opportunity to come back to put things right when we have departed from this world. Therefore, it is wise to make use of all the opportunities we have now in order to do things properly.

The past can hold a lot of shame and disappointment, but it depends on how we manage it. This is why it is difficult for many individuals to experience a bright future.

There is a story of a young woman who once attended an interview for a job. She got the job, but she failed to show up for her first day at work and did not even contact the employers. She went to work somewhere else, but it was not long before she lost that job. She tried other options, but it was not so easy for her to find another career. There came a time that she saw an advertisement for a vacancy in a particular place; but unfortunately, she could not apply for the job the second time, because it was the same place where she had previously failed to show up for work. Sometimes, we leave things behind in a very bad state and expect to return as if nothing was wrong.

The seeds we sow in the past can either help or hinder us. If the seeds we sow are bad, then we will surely reap a negative harvest. However, if we sow good seeds, then our harvest will be productive. Many families in the world have been torn apart as a result of issues of the past that were mismanaged without searching for a proper solution. Many men and women leave their marriages behind with nothing but grief because of certain issues from the past. Curses may have rained on many due to past indulgences. Nonetheless, by the grace of God, there is always an opportunity to change things.

Sins Of Our Fathers

There are acts our ancestors have committed in the past which have resulted in severe repercussions, and we wish we could go back in time to change things. Sometimes God allows us to become victims of bitter circumstances in order to chastise us so that we will learn to live a lifestyle that is pleasing to Him.

> *"It happened in the spring of the year, at the time when kings go out to battle, that David sent Joab and his servants with him, and all Israel; and they destroyed the people of Ammon and besieged Rabbah. But David remained at Jerusalem. Then it happened one evening that David arose from his bed and walked on the roof of the king's house. And from the roof he saw a woman bathing, and the woman was very beautiful to behold. So David sent and inquired about the woman, and someone said, 'Is this not Bathsheba, the daughter of Eliam, the wife of Uriah the Hittite?' Then David sent messengers, and took her; and she came to him, and he lay with her, for she was cleansed from her impurity; and she returned to her house."*
> [2 Samuel 11:1-4]

King David committed adultery with the wife of a man he knew. Bathsheba's husband, Uriah, was a neighbour and loyal servant to king David. Uriah never betrayed the king or offended him in anyway. Even David's servants reminded him that she was married. At this point, king David should have restrained himself from getting close to the woman.

He should have considered Uriah but his lust for Bathsheba overrode everything. It is easy to imagine the kind of thoughts that ran through David's mind as he sought after the woman, but it would also be easy to imagine the feelings of Uriah should he have ever discovered the truth about the king he faithfully served.

Questions:

Could it be that king David was not happy in his marriages and was looking for something that appeared to be better than what he already had?

Could it be that in all his splendour, the 'Great king of Israel' was still unfulfilled like a child looking for new toys to play with?

Was there not anyone strong and wise enough to advise David?

Was there not anyone who could have made him aware of his actions and the consequences he was going to experience?

Perhaps David pondered the consequences of his actions, or maybe he did not think twice about it. It could be that his own conscience made him aware of the evil that was about to unfold in his life, but the beauty of Bathsheba was too captivating. There is a possibility that he thought he had nothing to lose because of the great position he occupied.

Temptation has its way of blinding us to the point that we forget about the potential aftermath and how it can affect us. It has only one purpose and it is not something that we must flirt with, because it is the devil's way of causing our downfall. Sin only drags us into despair and takes us further away from God.

> *"And the woman conceived; so she sent and told David, and said, 'I am with child.' Then David sent to Joab, saying, 'Send me Uriah the Hittite.' And Joab sent Uriah to David. When Uriah had come to him, David asked how Joab was doing, and how the people were doing, and how the war prospered, and David said to Uriah, 'Go down to your house and wash your feet.'*
>
> *So Uriah departed from the king's house, and a gift of food from the king followed him. But Uriah slept at the door of the king's house with all the servants of his* Lord, *and did not go down to his house. So when they told David, saying, 'Uriah did not go down to his house,' David said to Uriah,*

'Did you not come from a journey? Why did you not go down to your house?' and Uriah said to David, 'The ark and Israel and Judah are dwelling in tents, and my LORD Joab and the servants of my LORD are encamped in the open fields. Shall I then go to my house to eat and drink, and to lie with my wife? As you live, and as your soul lives, I will not do this thing.'"

[2 Samuel 11:5-11]

King David knew exactly what he was doing; he did not even pause to consider the feelings of Uriah. In David's eyes, he had to get what he wanted regardless of who it belonged to.

Sometimes, the spirit of covetousness can be so strong that we can be oblivious to the effects of our actions. There are times that our desires and passions gain so much control over our minds that we become like robots. This is how we easily fall into the traps of temptation and become sorrowful victims of the devil. At this point, David still had the opportunity to change his mind and turn his life around, but he was too caught up in his wild imaginations. He was so mesmerised by Bathsheba's beauty. In fact, he forgot that God was watching everything he was doing. The power of sin can cause us to lose total focus on God and who we are almost as if God no longer exists. When we are too caught up in the desires of the flesh, we behave as if God is unconscious of our actions. However, He is always watching and hoping that we will choose to do His will and resist the devil.

"Then David said to Uriah, 'Wait here today also, and tomorrow I will let you depart.' So Uriah remained in Jerusalem that day and the next. Now when David called him, he ate and drank before him; and he made him drunk. And at evening he went out to lie on his bed with the servants of his LORD, but he did not go down to his house.

In the morning it happened that David wrote a letter to Joab and sent it by the hand of Uriah. And he wrote in the letter, saying, 'Set Uriah in the forefront of the hottest

> battle, and retreat from him, that he may be struck down and die.' So it was, while Joab besieged the city, that he assigned Uriah to a place where he knew there were valiant men. Then the men of the city came out and fought with Joab. And some of the people of the servants of David fell; and Uriah the Hittite died also."
>
> [2 Samuel 11:12-17]

David gave into the lust and became manipulative, a deceiver and conniver as the voice of his flesh spoke louder than ever. The spirit of lust turned David into his own enemy as he sank deeper into darkness.

Questions:

Can you identify with this situation?

Have you ever been so passionate about something you knew you were forbidden to have, but it was almost as if you did not care at all?

Have you ever found yourself in a place where you were never supposed to be, but it was almost as if you did not give a second thought about it?

Have you ever laid your hands on something you were not permitted to touch, but it felt so good to have it in the palm of your hands?

Perhaps you have set your eyes on some things that were a detriment to your soul, but somehow the consequences have not occurred to you yet. Maybe you have been engaging in some ungodly activities that have the potential to tear your destiny into pieces, but you have gone too deep to think twice about it. King David was fully aware of his unlawful intentions, but he chose not to resist temptation.

> "'The archers shot from the wall at your servants; and some of the king's servants are dead, and your servant

> Uriah the Hittite is dead also.' Then David said to the messenger, 'Thus you shall say to Joab: 'Do not let this thing displease you, for the sword devours one as well as another. Strengthen your attack against the city, and overthrow it.' So encourage him.'
>
> When the wife of Uriah heard that Uriah her husband was dead, she mourned for her husband, and when her mourning was over, David sent and brought her to his house, and she became his wife and bore him a son. But the thing that David had done displeased the LORD."
>
> [2 Samuel 11:24-27]

David did not have the legal right to be with Bathsheba, nevertheless he manipulated the situation to his advantage, and it ended in murder. It did not start out as his intention to murder Uriah, but that became expedient to avoid his sin becoming public. The desire to fulfil the lusts of his flesh turned into envy and bloodshed. David did not want his sin exposed - that is why he orchestrated Uriah's death.

Questions:

> *Why do we put ourselves in such positions considering that it can tear us to pieces?*
>
> *Why are we often very passionate about fulfilling the desires which only empowers and pleases the one who wants to destroy us - the devil?*

It could be that we have not yet come to full realisation that we have the power to conquer anything that is contrary to the supreme authority of God. God is the sovereign Lord who never fails, slumbers nor sleeps. We have what it takes to rise above every temptation regardless of what it is. By the grace of God, the power in us is greater than any power in the universe.

> "Then Nathan said to David, 'You are the man! Thus says the LORD God of Israel: I anointed you king over Israel,

> and I delivered you from the hand of Saul. I gave you your master's house and your master's wives into your keeping, and gave you the house of Israel and Judah. And if that had been too little, I also would have given you much more!
>
> Why have you despised the commandment of the LORD, to do evil in His sight? You have killed Uriah the Hittite with the sword; you have taken his wife to be your wife, and have killed him with the sword of the people of Ammon. Now therefore, the sword shall never depart from your house, because you have despised Me, and have taken the wife of Uriah the Hittite to be your wife.'
>
> Thus says the LORD: 'Behold, I will raise up adversity against you from your own house; and I will take your wives before your eyes and give them to your neighbour, and he shall lie with your wives in the sight of this sun. For you did it secretly, but I will do this thing before all Israel, before the sun'"
>
> [2 Samuel 12:7-12]

So God declared a curse against David and his family for his sins. Although David already had so much more than he could ever have imagined in his life, yet, his lack of satisfaction compelled him to take Uriah's wife. God specifically laid out David's punishment telling him exactly what would happen to him and his descendants. From that point, David was no longer the same; he knew he was going to experience some harrowing consequences because he ordered the death of an innocent man.

The Law Of Correction

When God implements discipline, it can often be very exacting, but we acknowledge that God's ways are perfect no matter how painful they may appear to be.

> "Now Absalom had commanded his servants, saying, "Watch now, when Amnon's heart is merry with wine,

and when I say to you, "Strike Amnon!" then kill him. Do not be afraid. Have I not commanded you? Be courageous and valiant.' So the servants of Absalom did to Amnon as Absalom had commanded. Then all the king's sons arose, and each one got on his mule and fled."

[2 Samuel 13:28-29]

The Lord never lies and He never goes back on His word; what he said against David is exactly what happened. It was certainly very painful for David to endure the evil consequences of his sins, but he had to go through it in order to learn the hard way.

His first son with Bathsheba died as a result of his sin.

His son Amnon raped his half-sister Tamar, David's daughter.

Absalom avenged the rape of Tamar and slew his half-brother, Amnon.

Later Absalom rose up against David, displaced him from the throne and publicly engaged in sexual acts with David's wives and concubines.

Absalom is later killed leading an uprising against David.

Adonijah, another of David's sons, had himself crowned, trying to usurp Solomon.

Following David's death, Solomon has Adonijah executed.

We can see that sexual immorality, strife and bloodshed were repeated in David's family because he committed adultery with Bathsheba and had shed Uriah's innocent blood.

Not all correction is as exacting as David's, but it is imperative to endure God's correction with humility; this is good for growth, and to reduce or eliminate error. The discipline of the Lord is a stepping stone to great achievements and is often used to break the pride in us. God's discipline provides guidance to those who are lost. The discipline of the Lord is a powerful teacher because it guides well. As spiritual soldiers, it is essential that we understand and fully acknowledge the necessity of pruning and purging in order to achieve perfection. [Hebrews 12:27-28] It is the plan of God that we all become perfect like Him, it starts in this life and will be completed when Christ comes for us. There are some painful trials and experiences that we must all go through so that God can establish His ways in us. This is why it necessary that we allow God to discipline us as He sees fit. God is constantly working on us; He wants to remove all the things that could possibly destroy us because He loves us.

It is the responsibility of the Shepherd to train the sheep because He knows what is best for the sheep. Just as the Shepherd loves the sheep, the sheep must love the Shepherd. We are the sheep who are fed, protected, loved, taught and guided by the Good Shepherd - Jesus. [John 10:11] He has the full authority to continually set us straight until we become like Him. Parents are earthly shepherds, and it is their responsibility to correct their children when necessary. There are many parents, guardians or teachers who fail to apply the correct type of discipline to produce positive results because they lack the experience and the right understanding.

Often in life, those who are supposed to be the teachers are the very ones who are in need of reproof. King David was a great teacher, but he also needed to be taught. No earthly teacher or leader knows it all. It is only God who knows and can do it all and He knows what is best for us.

Gaining Virtue From Experience

Life's experiences can be exceptional teachers; such events can guide us into the right places. Some episodes produce nothing but splendid memories which we automatically cherish. Some of the events in our lives only produce puzzling results which cause us to keep guessing. Some memories continue to give us headaches every time we are reminded of them.

Questions:

How have the occurrences in your life shaped you?

What valuable lessons have they taught you?

Have they equipped you with the correct knowledge and wisdom to lead you in the right direction?

Or, have they made you wish you had never been born?

It is important to understand that all the experiences in your life are profitable, regardless of how positive or painful they may be. Nevertheless, they can be a platform to stand on from which to reach out and grab what you are destined to possess.

In addition, your experiences are like telescopes that can enable you to catch a glimpse of your future in the sense that the things you go through can help you to discover your future. For example; Joseph saw his destiny in a dream and revealed it to his family. However, he went through many painful trials before that dream became a reality. The things he experienced gave Joseph a glimpse of what he was going to be.

Every occurrence in your life is very important; do not despise but cherish them because they are the blueprints to your destiny. Even the most challenging experiences from your past can become powerful testimonies. The achievements in your lifetime have the potential to inspire future generations. Truthfully speaking, your experiences may even be the perfect solution to many unanswered questions and an atlas to guide those who are lost. It is important to keep yourself in God's presence and His power, so that you will never wish you were not born.

You may have found yourself in a situation that caused you

to reflect - *'had I known, I would have prevented myself from going ahead with that ungodly thing I did yesterday. If only I could turn back the hands of time and go back to change things, I would have stopped myself from engaging in that abominable act some time ago. Had I known that I was going to experience such an extreme hardship, I would not have set my foot in that place. Had I known that God was going to allow shame and despair to have their way in my life, I would not have hurt that person some time ago. Had I known I was going to experience so much pain, I would not have looked at all those unclean things that I set my eyes on. Had I known that I was going to fall under such a curse, I would have chosen my friends more wisely.'*

> *"Now king David was old, advanced in years; and they put covers on him, but he could not get warm. Therefore his servants said to him, 'Let a young woman, a virgin, be sought for our* LORD *the king, and let her stand before the king, and let her care for him; and let her lie in your bosom, that our* LORD *the king may be warm.' So they sought for a lovely young woman throughout all the territory of Israel, and found Abishag the Shunammite, and brought her to the king. The young woman was very lovely; and she cared for the king, and served him; but the king did not know her."*
>
> [1 Kings 1:1-4]

Here we can see that David had learned his lesson; he refused to lay his hands on the young woman who was beside him. At this point, David had matured and gained the strength to resist the temptation of a young beautiful woman. It is important to learn from the mistakes of others so that we will not repeat the same mistakes.

Perhaps in your case, you wish you had not been late for that job interview. Maybe you are telling yourself - *'if only I treated her better, or if only I had treated him better, I would not be going through what I am going through now.'* Perhaps you are a pastor and you are wondering if you could turn back the hands of time and stop yourself from scattering the sheep.

The good news is that through Christ's sacrifice we can seek forgiveness and a new start to put right those areas of our lives in which we have failed. Thus, our descendants may not have to pay the price for our errors.

Juvenile delinquency, drug trafficking, gang warfare and so many other horrific occurrences continue to rise to devastating levels as a result of sins that were committed by certain people in the past. The sins we commit today, or have already committed, could possibly bring curses upon ourselves and our children, but we do not have to let that happen.

We can repent and allow God to break those generational bondages before it is too late. When we get things right, we will not have to go back to our yesterdays to identify the source of matters affecting us today and with the potential of ruining tomorrow. The prophet Daniel felt it was necessary to engage in prayer and fasting as a result of curses that fell upon his generation. [Daniel 9:1-27]

The curses occurred because of the sins of the ancestors of all the then current nation. The sins that were committed by relatives in the past have affected our generation in one way or another, especially as some refused to repent from their ungodly activities. Leaving the past behind can be very daunting, but if you desire to succeed, then you must be fully prepared to give up the very things in your past that have kept you complacent and bound for so long.

Chapter Five

Efficiency And Effectiveness

"Then God saw everything that He had made, and indeed it was very good. So the evening and the morning were the sixth day."

[Genesis 1:31]

The Clarity Of Efficiency And Effectiveness

Efficiency is the ability to generate something with a minimum amount of effort. Effectiveness is the measure to which objectives are accomplished and the magnitude to which difficult matters or situations are solved. Without the practice of efficiency and effectiveness, skills cannot be utilised proficiently and things will not be assembled properly. Thus, many purposes or results will never be achieved. It is important to have the expertise to compose or to construct something in an orderly fashion. There are many ways to be an efficient or effective individual.

You can be an efficient driver by controlling the consumption of fuel, as well as following the speed limit and obeying all road signs. The Word of God can help you to practice efficiency and teach you how to be effective. Many individuals and businesses across the globe have grown into great empires, and some have become exemplary figures to the world because of their healthy understanding of efficiency and effectiveness. An inefficient mind is a mind that is often confused and disorganised; therefore, such an individual becomes an ineffective person. Such a mind is the type that is most likely to struggle to put things together adequately and often fails to be successful. Therefore, it is important that we apply God's principles in everything we do in order to be productive in our accomplishments.

"God set them in the firmament of the heavens to give light on the earth, and to rule over the day and over the night, and to divide the light from the darkness. And God saw

that it was good."
[Genesis 1:17-18]

Whenever God created something, He saw that it was good. This is because God always does things according to wisdom. Efficiency and effectiveness are qualities that are very dear to God; it was through His meticulous mind that the two abilities originated. Through the Lord's creative and wonderful skill, He constructed the first man from the dust of the Earth. Again, we can see the effectiveness of that same skill repeated when God took one of his ribs and created a woman. The Bible tells us that, we are *"fearfully and wonderfully made"*. [Psalm 139:14] God made us with the power to multiply and be prosperous like Himself who is absolutely fruitful in all things. Nevertheless, God has given us a similar knowledge and skill to create masterpieces with our talents and gifts in order to reveal His power and infallible creativity to the world.

Know Your Purpose, Be Productive, Make A Difference, Be Somebody, Make History

Questions:

What have you achieved in your lifetime?

Are you really living the life that you are supposed to live?

If not, then what can you do to make a change?

Through observation, I have come to realise that a large number of Christians seem to be clueless about their purpose in life. It appears many Christians are convinced that they are only here to attend church and make money. God has imprinted something unique in all of us to make the world aware that we have all been created to fulfil a purpose before we die. Just as every person on Earth has a unique fingerprint, each human being has been ordained with a unique assignment. If you are oblivious to your purpose, then seek God's face and He will reveal it to you. But, if you are aware of it, then do not waste any more time and do not allow anything to hinder you from fulfilling your destiny. Also, if you are not sure, then ask the Holy Spirit to direct you because it is imperative that you do what God has placed you here to do.

> *"For the kingdom of heaven is like a man travelling to a far country, who called his own servants and delivered his goods to them. And to one he gave five talents, to another two, and to another one, to each according to his own ability; and immediately he went on a journey."*
> [Matthew 25:14-15]

God gives wonderful talents to everyone. He creates talents which suit each individual according to their calling and character. Every talent you have in your life corresponds with who you are; that is why it is important to acknowledge and appreciate who God created you to be. Nothing about you is a mistake, but the mistake is our inability to fully recognise the potential in us.

> *"And you shall take this rod in your hand, with which you shall do the signs."*
> [Exodus 4:17]

God placed a rod in Moses' hand. At first, he did not know how he was going to use the rod until God showed him how. God has put phenomenal things in each of our hands, and it is imperative that we learn to recognise their true value and power. Samson had a donkey's jawbone, but it was the power of the Holy Spirit upon him that made all the difference. Surely, a donkey's jawbone was not enough to fight against even a few men, but that did not matter because the Spirit of God made it enough to destroy a multitude of strong men. Therefore, the size of your talent or gift does not matter, especially when God is in control. David defeated Goliath by God's power with one stone. [1 Samuel 117:49-50]

The sling and stone seemed ineffective weapons to many

who were around - in comparison to Goliath whose physical stature and strength was a great threat to the nation of Israel. However, the miraculous power of God is what magnified the significance of the small stones in David's sling. God can use the seemingly most insignificant things in your life and turn them into the mightiest objects to His glory. God is more than able to make history out of the most ridiculous things. God can do the same with you if you avail yourself today; it is not about the size of what you have, as long as God determines the outcome. Is God not a wonderful God? Can He not cause miracles to happen in your life? Is He not more than able to turn nothing into something?

Self Development

In order to develop yourself or something properly, there must be a regular 'strategy of competence'. As you practice this attitude faithfully, you will gain the specified character that will determine the growth of your skill. It is evident that some learn more quickly than others do, but it all depends on the mentality of an individual. By this I mean that those who study and educate themselves with good knowledge are often the ones who succeed. But, those who do not dedicate themselves to acquiring the necessary knowledge are often the ones who fail to produce constructive results.

However, all human beings must experience a process of improvement in order to reach a certain level or to accomplish their assignment on earth. This is why most things in life involve a process or a journey. In order to produce something proficiently, it is important to apply knowledge and wisdom because it is impossible to create something if you do not know how to go about it. When God spoke the heavens, the earth and everything else into being, He used His infallible wisdom. [Genesis 1:31]

For example, God gave us eyebrows and eyelashes to protect our eyes and He placed our ears and noses in the best positions. If God had placed our noses upside down or our ears on top of our heads, they would fill to overflowing when it rains. God makes things for good reason. Therefore, as we produce, it is important that we also follow suit and do things wisely. Many Christians are not making adequate use of the power of productivity which God has freely given them.

Questions:

What are the things that prevent you from making good use of your talents?

What are some the weaknesses that prevent you from being efficient and effective in the Kingdom?

There are a number of reasons why people often fail to fulfil their destiny. It is imperative that the ways in which we can make good use of our talents and gifts are constructive.

As you discover the wonderful skills in you, you get to know and understand how they work. For example, babies must learn to crawl, speak, stand, walk, then they learn to run. Crawling helps little children to move from one place to another; learning to talk helps them to communicate with their parents and others around them. Learning to stand creates the opportunity for children to reach out for something that is beyond their grasp. Standing is also a sign that they are gaining strength in their legs, which also means they are growing up. Little children also learn to understand that walking is a method of transportation which moves them from one place to another, and learning to run helps them to move even faster.

Jesus was the Word of God so it stands to reason that He had to be what He was since *"God is not man that He should lie."* [Numbers 23:19] He thus became who He was ordained to be. Jesus spent a lot of His time in the presence of God and also with the elders in the temple; He educated Himself through the experience of the elders by asking and answering questions.

David experienced a unique process of development in the fields as a young shepherd. His greatest test of development was through his dangerous encounters with a fearsome lion and a gruesome bear. This gave David the necessary character and qualifications to be who God created him to be. In the same way, it is necessary to train yourself in the skills that will enable you to become who God has created you to be.

Developing yourself through the Word of God will enable you to gain the necessary character to produce whatever it is you have been assigned to produce with your skill.

> "Then Peter opened his mouth and said: 'In truth I perceive that God shows no partiality.'"
>
> [Acts 10:34]

Scripture tells us that God is not a respecter of persons; He does not focus on our imperfections, qualifications or our status. God specially selected David who was an unpopular boy in the wilderness and turned him into a mighty king. Gideon was a simple man but God selected him out of a multitude and transformed him into a great deliverer. [Judges 6-7] God can do the same with you if you humble yourself before Him. By His grace, God can use whoever He chooses regardless of whom or what that person is. God does not look at the richest or the most intelligent person on earth because there is no such thing in the eyes of God. We all need to seek the necessary wisdom in order to understand the importance of the abilities in us.

The Lord is waiting to see what we will do with the mysteries He has hidden in us. It is of paramount importance to be fully diligent in making use of the skills that God has invested in us. We cannot afford to fail God, as there are many lives waiting to be touched and transformed by our talents and gifts. Therefore, let us all utilise the Divine endowments in our lives to make the world a better place.

The Power Of Influence

In life, there are dream killers and destiny breakers. There are also, dream makers and destiny angels. The dream killers are those who will do their best to fight against you and to persuade you to neglect your talents. Nevertheless, there are those who will find absolute joy in helping you cultivate your dream even to the extent of working harder on your dream than you might be inclined to do. The destiny breakers are the ones who want to destroy you completely. Some may even attempt to kill you, such was the case with Abel who lived a very short life because his brother Cain brutally murdered him out of envy. [Genesis 4:8]

However, the destiny angels are the ones whom God assigns to guide, protect, defend, correct, encourage you, polish, strengthen, humble, pray and fight for you, and make sure that you fulfil your purpose. Evaluate yourself daily, so that you also will not become a dream killer or destiny breaker. This is because there are certain weaknesses in you that could be hazardous to you or others around you. Be watchful that you do not allow any negative experiences to cause you to hate others no matter how disapproving they appear to be. This is because there are some who genuinely want to help you, but circumstances lead to their disappointing you along the way.

It is very important to have healthy support from the right people - those who will appreciate your work and will go through the struggle with you. Such individuals are your allies; they are the ones who will understand the importance of your talents and will help you to reach where your creativity is destined to take you. Many individuals are falling behind in producing the things their skills are designed to yield because they do not have the support they need. Not everyone will embrace your skill irrespective of how significant it is.

There are those who will think your talent is of no use, but it is because they lack understanding. Nevertheless, despite what others may think, it is imperative to be passionate about your talents because they are much greater than you can comprehend. If you fail to acknowledge the power of your abilities, then you will disappoint God. [Matthew 25:24-30]

Ignorance

Many have failed to succeed because they have allowed the spirit of ignorance to overtake their minds. This attitude often leads to failure and misdirection. This seems to happen when people do not know or understand the weight of their purpose. This type of mentality has affected a colossal number of believers and has persuaded many to presume that their talents are not as inspiring as those of others. Therefore, they tend to underestimate the significance of their endowments. As much as some have recognised their priceless abilities, all the same, they may at times misuse the power of their skills because they do not know who they are.

Life is not about doing the will of man, but doing the will of God. It is critical to recognise that your life is not about what people think or say; it is not about what others expect you to be. Rather, your life is about how you can fulfil God's purpose in this world before you depart, since your aim must be to please God and not men. [Galatians 1:10] All humans in the world are gifted; some are lamentably failing to live up to their potential because of the pernicious influences around them. I have seen too many people whose gifts have been woefully misused or neglected because they are not even aware that they need to manage their gifts.

The failure of an individual can be more than enough to devastate a whole generation. But, you have the perfect opportunity to make a significant change so that you will be a great blessing to your generation. The choices you make today can historically impact the world for centuries. This is a God-given occasion for you to take the initiative, eradicate every bad influence in your life and boldly walk on the path to success. By the grace of God, you have another viable prospect to see your life from God's point of view and understand why it is so important that you live the life God created for you.

God created you to be fruitful and multiply. Fruitfulness is not limited to procreation, God also expects us to produce good results. God never lies and He cannot go against His Word. God did not create you to be imprisoned in a corner or lack the power to succeed. You are exceptional and expected to achieve much. This is why it is crucial that you refuse to compromise or settle for less. The enemy is very good at using the challenges around you to exasperate your mind. In doing so, he can convince you to think you are not qualified to achieve anything at all. In addition, you have the potential to make a difference because you have the calibre to show forth God's glory through your achievements.

Life can be deplorable, especially when circumstances seem to conspire to convince you to think that you are not good enough. You also begin to tell yourself that you are not 'tough, clever or beautiful enough.' It is important to realise that you do not need to be handsome or popular to qualify. Stop telling yourself that it will take too long or you are too old or too young. Stop letting others tell you that 'you are not experienced enough, your time has not come yet, or it is too late.' It is not up to people to tell you that you are not ready, your time has passed; or that you may end up like your brother or sister, or your father and mother who shamefully failed. You have what it takes to rise above it all and get to the finish line. It is necessary to remember that you have special abilities that make you irreplaceable - the phenomenon in you cannot be created by any human being on earth. Gather the necessary boldness; march forward and use your gifts to transform your generation.

Sometimes, the voices of pride and ignorance can utter so many foolish things to poison your mind. It is the enemy's plan to make you think you are alright where you are as if there is nothing else to be done. You might tell yourself 'It is well'. It is good to say this, but it is better to act, so that your assignment in God will come to pass. No circumstance has the right to determine your destiny; no human being has the right to map out your purpose for you. Remember what God has said about you. You are so much more than you can ever imagine; there is no one on earth who is exactly like you. You are the only one who can be you. No human being in the world has the fingerprints and the features that you have. No matter how much you may resemble another person, you are unquestionably unique.

Remember, even twins do not have the same features– mentally and physically. Thus, begin to recognise the promises that God has declared upon you and understand that He has already endowed you with everything you need to prosper.

The Lord has equipped you with 'supernatural intelligence' - more than enough to pass every test. Assure yourself that, you have these things in you to push you in the right direction. Consequently, the most important thing is to fix your mind on Christ daily and let your whole life be dedicated to Him. God could have decided not to create you, but He thought of you and put you together. He could have ended your life a long time ago; He could have selected another individual to fit in your shoes, but He chose you instead. God left His Throne of grace and came to shed His blood for you. Christ died, so that you will have the freedom to live the life He orchestrated for you. Think about this very carefully! Therefore, let the excellent mind of Christ be in you, so that you may fully comprehend and highly esteem the calling of God in you. The endeavour you undertake today can either be a tool of deliverance for yourself and others or it can be a weapon of destruction to yourself and others.

Consider the story of the *"prodigal son"* who decided to leave his father's house and go into the world to enjoy his life. He spent all his riches with harlots and other so-called friends and failed to make good use of his inheritance. [Luke 15:11-32]

The word 'prodigal' has a number of meanings such as irresponsible, undisciplined, out of control, extravagant, reckless, impatient, immature and inexperienced. The prodigal son was reckless with his inheritance because of his ignorance and lack of experience. Many prodigals fail to produce something significant with the wonderful talents they have because they are not as responsible as they should be.

Like a baby with a brand new toy, it is very likely that the toy will eventually be broken into pieces as the baby is not fully aware of the cost of the toy. This is why we need the necessary wisdom and the right character.

> "Then He said: 'A certain man had two sons, and the younger of them said to his father, 'Father, give me the portion of goods that falls to me.' So he divided to them his livelihood. And not many days after, the younger son gathered all together, journeyed to a far country, and there wasted his possessions with prodigal living. But when he had spent all, there arose a severe famine in that land, and he began to be in want. Then he went and joined himself to a citizen of that country, and he sent him into his fields to feed swine. And he would gladly have filled his stomach with the pods that the swine ate, and no one gave him anything.'"
>
> [Luke 15:11-16]

We know from the Bible what the prodigal son experienced and the lesson he learned. If you choose to be reckless with the treasure in you, then you will surely inherit the payback that is suitable for your carelessness. The prodigal son had everything he needed in life when he was in his father's house; he was surrounded by his family and many servants, yet he left the house. There are many who tend to think there is something better out there in the world than in the Kingdom of God. In addition, you must not allow your God-given abilities to be revealed to the wrong people; they will only convince you to misuse your gifts.

As the prodigal son took his inheritance and went into the midst of the wrong crowd, he failed to be the person he was supposed to be. As he squandered a very important investment that could have turned him into a very powerful person, he fell into shame. However, he had the opportunity to start again when he realised his mistake and went back home. Your God-given talent can turn you into a powerful individual–if and when you utilise it according to God's guidance. Nevertheless, if you choose to live a life that is contrary to God, then you must expect nothing but failure. Your skills have the power to change the world; therefore, be as creative as you can be. Be as useful to the Kingdom of God as you can be; but most of all, be as wise as you can be, your talents are more precious than you could ever imagine.

The Significance Of Skill

Since my childhood, I have noticed that many people give more acclaim to lawyers, doctors, accountants or those with white-collar jobs; yet they find it difficult to acknowledge the importance of such jobs as artisans, farmers, soldiers and nurses. This is because they believe that their skills are more significant. This mentality just encourages individuals to think that any other talent as a waste. It has caused many people to dishonour God because they often believe that white-collar jobs are the only occupations that are worthwhile, yet where would we be if the refuse bins were not emptied?

Through this mind-set, many are neglecting their true talents. This has also caused many to believe that they can only be successful if they practice so-called 'white-collar skills.' Are doctors not in need of houses to live in which builders construct? Do lawyers have the capability to nurse the sick? Are accountants not in need of food to eat which farmers cultivate? Do they not need offices to work in, chairs to sit on and desks to work on, all of which are made by carpenters?

Paul was a tent maker as well as a proclaimer and teacher of the Gospel:

> "So, because he was of the same trade, he stayed with them and worked; for by occupation they were tent-makers."
>
> [Acts 18:3]

In many ways, Paul's occupation as a tent-maker was not a focal point, because of his calling to spread the gospel. We can identify the significant impact Paul made in his lifetime and still does today.

> "Luke the beloved physician and Demas greet you. Greet the brethren who are in Laodicea, and Nymphas and the church that is in his house."
>
> [Colossians 4:14-15]

We see that Luke was a medical doctor as well as a disciple of Jesus Christ. I do not know how successful Luke was as a doctor, but it is evident that he was a very prominent teacher of the Gospel as were Matthew and Paul. Luke is certainly among the greatest names in the Bible - not for his medical profession, but for his diligence in the Kingdom. Proclaiming Jesus to the world was what gave Luke his public stature. His teachings of the Lord have become a great source of wisdom and instruction continuing to us today. Your worldly career cannot match up to your legacy in the Lord.

> "As Jesus passed on from there, He saw a man named Matthew sitting at the tax office, and He said to him, 'Follow Me.' So he arose and followed Him."
>
> [Matthew 9:9]

Matthew's occupation was a tax collector. Tax collectors were often not in people's good books, because they collected money even from the poor. However, we know of him as a close disciple and gospel author. Matthew, Luke and Paul all had one thing in common, they were all powerful men of God whom Jesus appointed to teach the Gospel. Would it be right to say that both Paul and Matthew were of no significance because they were not medical doctors as Luke was? Nevertheless, God gave all three the opportunity to be equal in one special area - they all became great men of God.

Whoever you are, do not allow the unique talents in you to be downsized or compared to others. Do not look at your abilities as if they are not as great as your neighbour's endowment. All talents and gifts are equal in the sight of the Lord.

Moreover, there are many artisans, street cleaners, labourers and farmers as well as others who often disregard white-collar skills, because they perceive that such occupations are only for the slothful. Some often disrespect bureaucrats, bank managers and business entrepreneurs because they do not acknowledge them as hard workers. This is due to the wrong perception of individuals who only believe that those who use their hands to scrub the floors, sweep the streets or lift heavy goods, are the significant workers. Golfers, dancers, designers, newsreaders, actors, authors and others have been criticised by some, because many do not recognise such people as hard workers. These and others like them perform difficult tasks daily in order to earn an income. Not all of us can sit in front of a camera all day to read the news, and not all human beings have the expertise to strike tiny balls into tiny holes with a very slim club.

Not all of us can skilfully cut fabric from which to make clothes. Not all of us can answer phone calls all day, manage confidential files and business empires like some can. Some have stated that teachers just stand in front of their students in the classroom and talk. But, teaching is a very talented capability. Also, it takes a lot of courage, patience, intelligence, and wisdom to teach others. Teachers have a lot to deal with, especially when their students are very wayward. You can be a hard worker in the office and you can be hard working on the street, in a kitchen or on a farm. Some jobs can be very dirty whilst other occupations require complete neatness, especially in corporate establishments.

Nevertheless, every skill is significant for its purpose despite what it is or what it involves. One can be a hard worker as a taxi driver and another can be a hard worker as a hairdresser or a barber. One can be diligent in singing and another can be very productive as a guitarist.

Everything we do first develops in our minds. Some talents require a much larger percentage of the use of hands and feet, whilst other skills require a greater use of mental agility. Actors memorise scripts in their minds and perform in theatres, on television and in films. Musicians apply their hands and feet to play instruments, or utilise their mouths to play instruments such as trumpets, flutes, and saxophones. Singers use their voices to express songs to listeners. Business entrepreneurs and designers create intricate ideas in their minds and use their communication skills to trade. Dancers use their limbs and their bodies to demonstrate complex choreography which they create in their minds.

The Pilot And The Mechanic

This is a story which illustrates how mindsets can be changed; it is about a mechanic and a pilot. One morning, on his way to a very important meeting, the pilot's vehicle broke down even though it was a very luxurious car. Fortunately, he found a mechanic who assessed the situation. As the mechanic began to make use of his skills, the pilot was astonished at his professionalism and he commented:

> *"It must be a miracle. I had no idea that vehicle mechanics were this sharp compared to aircraft engineers, but you seem so educated. Have you seen an aircraft engine before?"*

He ignorantly assumed that the vehicle mechanic was an illiterate. The mechanic answered:

> *"The fancy suit you wear does not mean anything to me at all. Besides, you pilots don't know what it means to work hard*

> anyway: all you do is just sit comfortably in the cockpits and fly airplanes; it's just like driving a giant, fancy car through mid-air. Don't you just sit back, relax and let the auto-pilot do all the hard work?"

The pilot retorted:

> "Yes it's true that we pilots sit in the cockpit and fly planes; however, we have responsibilities that you vehicle mechanics cannot imagine. Firstly, we are responsible for all the passengers on the plane. Secondly, I personally have manoeuvred aircraft through treacherous storms and landed in the ocean from about thirty thousand feet in the air–at the speed of almost six hundred miles per hour. Not to mention all the other technicalities involved. Many good pilots have lost their lives doing this. And, as for the auto-pilot, it is very necessary because it can pilot an airplane more accurately, and it does not get tired.
>
> Recently, I was forced to perform an emergency landing in a remote area due to an engine failure. A vast number of the passengers did not survive the crash, and the rest sustained severe injuries including myself.
>
> My co-pilot did not make it to the hospital alive; it could have been me. In that same week, I lost a colleague whose airline crashed into a forest, and killed every person on board."

The mechanic answered in astonishment:

> "That's frightening; I don't think I could handle the thought of knowing that innocent people could lose their lives through a crash in my vehicle. It must be very difficult to see many good people die.
>
> You know, I'm glad we're having this conversation, as I can already see what you go through each time you go to work. To leave your family behind and travel thousands of miles through the skies into unfamiliar territories and not knowing whether you will get back home alive. Taking those extreme measures each day seems very difficult for one person to handle; I don't

think I could ever do your job."

The pilot replied:

"I respect your intelligence, and I admire your hard work. I've seen how professional you are. Considering the injuries you must get on your hands, and the aches and pains you get, I'm amazed that you still do your job with such determination. I admire your work."

The mechanic replied:

"I trained and qualified at a very good college; in fact, I aim to own my own car company to design and manufacture better vehicles."

The pilot answered:

"I believe you can make it if you work hard on it; plus, you have the right attitude and you are smart too. As a matter of fact, I know just the right people who may help you to establish that business."

The mechanic replied:

"How can I refuse such an offer? It has always been my dream and my passion. I am very grateful; God bless you."

The pilot answered:

"You're welcome, Sir."

This is a wonderful illustration to help us understand that every skill carries its responsibilities regardless of what it is. We are all created for a unique purpose. Making use of the special ability in you is crucial. Every skill in you is essential; it is important to appreciate all your abilities and acknowledge that God gave them to you. Therefore, be grateful for what you are good at; it has much greater potential than you might envisage.

Chapter Six

Use Your Talents To Build God's Kingdom

> *"Then the* LORD *spoke to Moses, saying: 'See, I have called by name Bezalel the son of Uri, the son of Hur, of the tribe of Judah. And I have filled him with the Spirit of God, in wisdom, in understanding, in knowledge, and in all manner of workmanship, to design artistic works, to work in gold, in silver, in bronze, in cutting jewels for setting, in carving wood, and to work in all manner of workmanship.'"*
>
> [Exodus 31:1-5]

In the Old Testament, God instructed the children of Israel to build the Tabernacle in a specific way. The Lord gave the people unique talents, so that together they could create the structure according to God's specifications. If you try to utilise your talent using a method that is not of God, you will experience serious difficulties.

It is plain to see that God was present and very involved in the lives of the Israelites and He blessed them with unique gifts. You have no reason to think that you do not have any skill to put anything together. The scripture proves that God has put a specific assignment in every human being to do something that will bring glory to His name.

> *"The tabernacle of meeting, the ark of the Testimony and the mercy seat that is on it, and all the furniture of the tabernacle - the table and its utensils, the pure gold lampstand with all its utensils, the altar of incense, the altar of burnt offering with all its utensils, and the laver and its base - the garments of ministry, the holy garments for Aaron the priest and the garments of his sons, to minister as priests, and the anointing oil and sweet incense for the holy place. According to all that I have commanded you they shall do."*
>
> [Exodus 31:6-11]

We can clearly see that God is very creative; He is a true

Master of design and construction. According to the Bible passage, some of the Israelites who built the Tabernacle were goldsmiths and silversmiths. Some were skilled sculptors, while others were highly gifted in clothing design. We can also see in other areas that some of the children of Israel were instrumentalists and singers; and, even Aaron the high priest was a mouthpiece for Moses. [Exodus 4:15-16] Most importantly, we notice that all the skills of the Israelites were endowed for the sake of the Tabernacle.

Many wonderful skills are revealed to us throughout the Bible. Some were farmers, scribes, watchmen, teachers, shepherds, blacksmiths, builders and others. However, it was God who endows us with all these wonderful skills to be used for His glory.

Perhaps you have discovered a hidden passion for a musical instrument, but you are not confident enough to practice it. Could it be that you have the desire to be useful in the clothing industry, but you think it is too late for you. It could be that you have a unique love for sports, but you are not prepared to take on the challenge to get involved. Whatever skill is buried in you, it is important to gather the necessary courage to express that unique ability. Perhaps, you can use your creative skill to decorate your place of worship. You can use your love for sports to set up a fitness group with your Christian brethren. If you have a passion for music, let the Holy Spirit teach you how to play instruments for the Kingdom. Any expertise that is buried in you is already useful to God and He will appreciate your labour of love in developing it.

Appreciate your talent; be confident in your creativity and let it shine throughout the world. It pleases God when we totally throw ourselves into our skills and special abilities. God designed your skills and they are very dear to His heart; therefore, do not allow your attitude to cause God to declare you to be a wicked and slothful servant. [Matthew 25:25-30] When you do your best and make good use of what the Lord has placed in you, you will surely enter into the *"joy of the Lord"*. [Matthew 25:23]

Fear Of Failure

There are two types of people in this world. Firstly, there are those who boldly go through the wilderness, and beyond to achieve the impossible. Secondly, there are those who only sit back and choose to receive from others because they are often too afraid to try for themselves. This mentality is causing many believers to deteriorate in the Kingdom, because they are not convinced that God has already provided them with all the power and knowledge they need.

> *"Behold, I give you the authority to trample on serpents and scorpions, and over all the power of the enemy, and nothing shall by any means hurt you."*
> [Luke 10:19]

By this, we are made aware that God has empowered us to have dominion over everything, but very often we fail to remember who we are. Being afraid to embark on the necessary journey toward your destiny will not produce any constructive results; it will only oppress you and push you down into the belly of failure. The fear of the unknown has become a stronghold in the minds of believers, especially when individuals spend too much time pondering the difficulties they may face along the way.

> *"Yea, though I walk through the valley of the shadow of death, I will fear no evil; For You are with me; Your rod and Your staff, they comfort me."*
> [Psalm 23:4]

In this Bible passage, David strengthened himself by saying he would fear no evil. Walking in the valley of the shadow of death is an indication that David was aware of his many enemies and their plans towards him. David could have allowed the spirit of fear to rule his mind, but he did not. In cases such as this, many give up their dreams because they become too paranoid about what could happen if they make certain decisions. On the other hand, there are multitudes of people in the world who have broken ranks and are enjoying their victory because they refused to be afraid of potential challenges.

Moses was a great man of God, but at first he was afraid of his assignment because of his speech impediment. But God straightened him out, encouraged him and gave him the ability to overcome that weakness. [Exodus 3] Sometimes, our defects can persuade us to look down on ourselves as if we are not capable enough to do what God created us to do. This is one of the many ways that the spirit of fear can prevent us from marching on like giants.

> *"And the Spirit of the LORD came mightily upon him, and he tore the lion apart as one would have torn apart a young goat, though he had nothing in his hand. But he did not tell his father or his mother what he had done."*
> [Judges 14:6-7]

We can see that Samson chose to exercise faith in God. He could have turned back, but as the Spirit of the Lord came upon him, his enormous courage erupted and he slew the lion. In the Bible passage, you will notice that Samson killed the lion after the Spirit of the Lord came upon him. This is to help us realise that we already have what it takes to conquer anything that can potentially tear us apart because the Holy Ghost is here to help us. We disappoint God when we allow the spirit of fear to overpower us. This is because we already have the power that is greater than every other power and yet we often fail to use it. When you begin to understand that *"He that is in you is greater than he that is in the world"* [1 John 4:4] you will conquer. He who dwells in you is fearless and fearsome - even more than anything in the universe.

The Power Of Prayer

For a number of years, I discovered that many believers already have full knowledge of their talents and unique gifts, but they do not know how to put them into practice. In addition, I concluded that some do not engage in the kind of prayer that releases the support they need from God. Many Christians do not pray about their talents and gifts, because they do not believe in themselves as much as they should. The Apostle Paul advised Timothy to engage in spiritual warfare in order to manifest all the prophecies that were proclaimed upon him. Paul understood the importance of prayer. [1 Timothy 1:18] In fact, some do not pray because they are afraid that God will not respond. However, failure to pray can result in some dire consequences.

In the Bible, we are told that king Herod apprehended James the brother of John and murdered him. [Acts 12:1-2] However, we are also told that when Peter was arrested and imprisoned by king Herod, the Church prayed and an angel of the Lord was sent to rescue him from prison.

> *"Peter was therefore kept in prison, but constant prayer was offered to God for him by the church. And when Herod was about to bring him out, that night Peter was sleeping, bound with two chains between two soldiers; and the guards before the door were keeping the prison. Now behold, an angel of the LORD stood by him, and a light shone in the prison; and he struck Peter on the side and raised him up, saying, 'Arise quickly!' And his chains fell off his hands. Then the angel said to him, 'Gird yourself and tie on your sandals;' and so he did. And he said to him, 'Put on your garment and follow me.'"*
> [Acts 12:1-8]

By this Biblical account, we can see the wonderful effects of prayer and the benefits of it. Lack of prayer can turn you into a victim; it can prevent you from experiencing the glory of the Lord. In your case, the 'king Herod' in your life could be anything that has the potential to destroy you. Perhaps, the situation in your life has killed your confidence just as Herod killed James. However, be reminded that, you already have what it takes to break the curse of every Herod in your life. Sometimes, circumstances can convince us that we will never succeed in anything at all, especially when we do not feel strong enough to fight. Therefore, we allow the fear of failure to confuse us and in turn, it prevents us from fulfilling our purpose in God. Some fail to pray because they are afraid of the devil's attacks.

It is crucial to accept that God has not given us the spirit of fear. [2 Timothy 1:7] What God has placed in us is more than enough to demolish every stronghold. We must not take the power of God for granted, because it is the power above all powers. There are people who take the back seat and criticise others who are making a difference with their talents because they themselves lack the boldness to fight. However, you have the opportunity to make a great impression on those who lack understanding. In doing so, the wonders of your talent will inspire them to make changes in their own lives.

The Importance Of Being Honourable

Greatness is only a prayer away, but there are some important factors that must be understood. God has prepared an opportunity so wide that, it would take centuries for it to run out because it will continue to benefit your generation after you are dead and gone. However, there are rules that must be followed in order to maintain that opportunity. As long as we are alive, God expects us to be honourable to Him and to one another.

> *"Now Jabez was more honourable than his brothers, and his mother called his name Jabez, saying, 'Because I bore him in pain.' and Jabez called on the God of Israel saying, 'Oh, that You would bless me indeed, and enlarge my territory, that Your hand would be with me, and that You would keep me from evil, that I may not cause pain!' so*

God granted him what he requested."
[1 Chronicles 4:9-10]

Jabez was under a curse and it seemed almost impossible for any wonders to manifest in his life. However, the Bible tells us that Jabez was more honourable than his brothers. Therefore, when he lifted his eyes onto the Lord and opened his mouth in prayer, God answered him and delivered him from the curse that was resident in his family. At this time of your life, the key to your breakthrough is to remain as honourable as possible because that is what will persuade God to break down every evil stronghold in your life.

Question:

What does it mean to be honourable and why is it important?

To be honourable is to be respectable, responsible, principled, and maintain the moral conduct. It means being obedient to God and practising holiness and righteousness.

Being honourable is to help the poor.

Being honourable is not to point fingers at people or make false accusations.

It is to forgive others for their mistakes and accept God's forgiveness for yourself. In addition, to be honourable is to be prayerful and to be thankful to God.

To refrain from activities that satisfy the flesh.

It is to pay your tithes and offerings.

It it is to acknowledge your mistakes and be accountable for your actions.

It is important to remain honourable in the sight of the Lord because that is what pleases Him. Jesus modelled this way of life for us until the day He ascended to Heaven. That is what made Jesus so pure and so powerful beyond what any human being could ever imagine.

> *"So Hannah arose after they had finished eating and drinking in Shiloh. Now Eli the priest was sitting on the seat by the doorpost of the tabernacle of the LORD. And she was in bitterness of soul, and prayed to the LORD and wept in anguish. Then she made a vow and said, 'O LORD of hosts, if You will indeed look on the affliction of Your maidservant and remember me, and not forget Your maidservant, but will give Your maidservant a male child, then I will give him to the LORD all the days of his life, and no razor shall come upon his head.'"*
>
> [1 Samuel 1:9-11]

We can clearly see how Hannah maintained her dignity and honour in the sight of the Lord in spite of her predicament. She did not lose her composure and she did not blaspheme or curse God. Despite the reproach in her life, she did not limit her duties to the Lord. It is plain to see that Hannah did not compromise on her relationship with God no matter how shameful her life appeared to be. In some cases, there are women who have gone ahead and committed adultery in order to conceive, especially when it appeared that the fault lay with their husbands. Hannah could have started drinking; she could have started to misbehave in order to get her way, but she did not do so. Also, we can see that she did not fight against God in spite of her condition. She could have given up on her marriage as a result of the challenges she had to endure.

Hannah could have complained to everybody about the problems she faced, but she remained honourable. Truthfully speaking, many women would have attempted to fight the other woman or tried to drive her out. Hannah could have tried to 'cause confusion' between Peninnah, the other wife of Elkanah, their husband, but she maintained her integrity. [1 Samuel 1:1-2] In fact, she could have tried to murder Peninnah, or even thought of committing suicide, but she remained acquiescent to the Lord, regardless of the indignity she experienced. She could have tried many other solutions and perhaps, even gone ahead to consult other gods for help, but she remained faithful to her Maker. Therefore, when she prayed, God could not deny her. In fact, Hannah's prayer was the kind of prayer that really persuades God to do wonders.

Hannah did not take her situation lightly. The day she stood firm and poured her heart out to God, something miraculous took place.

Prayer has the potential to destroy evil and open impossible doors, but being honourable is what will qualify you to experience breakthrough. When God remembered Hannah and blessed her with Samuel, she honoured God to an even greater height. She kept her promise to God and offered her baby as a gift to the Lord. This is what persuaded God to do even greater things in Hannah's life. To this day, her name is among the greatest in the history of God's people because of her honourable attitude towards God. Being honourable can map out your destiny, qualify you to be delivered from ancestral curses and launch you into the abundance of the Lord. [1 Samuel 2:21,26]

Slothfulness

> *"The lazy man does not roast what he took in hunting, But diligence is man's precious possession."*
> [Proverbs 12:27]

Too much complacency can cause delay and despair in your life. If you continue to rest on your laurels, or become complacent, then it will be difficult for you to succeed. [Proverbs 13:4] It is important to do your best to use your area of expertise to make a difference. Sacrifice your comforts today and begin the journey of discovering your strong points and use them to get to your 'Promised Land'. It is time for you to reach out and enjoy a taste of the success that God has ordained for you. It is not about how many times you try, but how relentless you are. You must understand that, if you really want to succeed, you will need to calculate what you are willing to give up in order to reach where you are meant to be. Slothfulness makes it difficult to sacrifice the things we must eliminate.

> *"Do you see a man who excels in his work? He will stand before kings; he will not stand before unknown men."*
> [Proverbs 22:29]

Lack of diligence is a 'disease' that has infected so many people, causing them to fail in many ways. Procrastination often takes away the opportunities that are before us; we often tell ourselves - *"I will do it later"*, *"I will go when the time comes"*, *"let me do something else first"*, *"I'll do it when I'm in the mood"* or *"let me rest a little; I will go when I finish resting"*. This mentality will only continue to keep us in darkness. It takes away the passion to propel us; it also prevents us from being ushered into the presence of kings. [Proverbs 22:29]

When the spirit of depression steps in, it can take away every positive inspiration in your life and replace it with doubt, fear, and deprivation. It is imperative to remind ourselves that we can never regain all the time we have lost or wasted because it is impossible to turn back the hands of time. Therefore, make use of the opportunities you have now, so that you can make a difference. Rise up out of your comfort zone and go where God is expecting you to go–to do what God expects of you.

In the book of Ruth, two widows experienced a heartbreaking situation - they both lost their husbands at the same time. In all of this, they had to make a decision about what to do to survive. Stranded with their mother-in-law in the middle of nowhere, Ruth and Orpah had to make a choice to push forward or go back home to their families. Going back meant that they would return to nothing, which was where their journey had begun. Ruth was the only one who was strong enough and moved forward to achieve her ultimate goal.

This was a result of her diligent spirit. Ruth did not allow the predicament she was in to overshadow her future.

The other widow, Orpah, decided to go back to where she came from, but that is where her story ends. By contrast, Ruth took the bold step and went to Bethlehem with her mother-in-law, only to discover that her destiny was there waiting to embrace her. It is obvious that Ruth experienced a lot of pain and sorrow when she lost her husband, but she rose above that pain. She worked relentlessly to glean crops and she made use of her substance from morning to evening without a complaint. In addition, she showed no sign of defeat. This attitude qualified her to gain favour with Boaz who was a wealthy businessman and the proprietor of the land she gleaned. Eventually, Boaz became the replacement for Ruth's dead husband. This was a wonderful compensation. [Ruth 4:13]

Questions:

What would have happened if Ruth was slothful in taking the bold step to follow her mother-in-law?

Would Boaz have noticed her if she allowed her circumstances to pull her back to where she started?

If Ruth had not gone with Naomi, she would not have discovered that God had made provision for her in that land. Slothfulness only draws us back and causes us to remain in the same spot which, in turn, deprives us of the resources God has ready and waiting for us. However, diligence will always drive us to where God wants us to go and will definitely help us to experience the blessings that are available to us. Ruth could have used her situation as an excuse to relax, or to gain sympathy and attention. She could have shrunk back in fear and doubt, but she did not allow that idea to dominate her mind.

In addition, she kept herself busy by working hard from morning to evening. That morning to evening period represents the length of time it takes for our breakthrough to appear. For some, it could be one or two years and for some it could be more, but our consistency is what will make the difference. Ruth's faithfulness was the key that opened the door to her destiny; she became the great grandmother of king David.

Questions:

So, what choice are you going to make?

Will you allow the spirit of slothfulness to slow you down and prevent you from stepping into glory?

Will you use this book as an inspiration to help usher you into your destiny?

Be diligent, according to the will of God, and you shall surely stand before kings and be among the greatest people. Such was the life of Christ; because of His diligent service to the Father, He is now seated at the right hand of power. Jesus Christ is now and always will be the greatest and most Sovereign King of all. Therefore, it is through Christ that we can gain the necessary passion to be diligent disciples. By doing so, we will stand before leaders and be in the category of the exceptional. It is of paramount importance to possess the ability to overcome every obstacle and limitation.

Sometimes people fail to achieve their goals because they expect to reap a harvest as soon as they plant their seeds. Some are blessed to reap after just a short while; but for others, it takes years of toiling and many trials before they experience a little success. However, many suffer the disease of not trying hard enough and some do not make an attempt at all, because they are afraid of losing the comfort they have.

Sometimes it is not because people do not do the right thing, but it is because they do not do the right thing long enough to produce the right results. When you make up your mind and stand firm, then God's providence will enable you to accomplish your purpose. Therefore, I tell you today that you will get there by the leading of the Holy Spirit. It has never been easy and it will not get any easier, but as long as God is alive, all you need to do is to 'keep on keeping on' and God will do all the rest. Remember, there is nothing too difficult for the Lord. [Genesis18:14]

Pride And Misdirection

Sometimes we try to tell God what we think we ought to be and should have. Adam was gifted as a gardener, but he did not tell God what he thought He should do.

When God created Adam, He gave him the ability to envisage with his mind and the knowledge to create - though obviously not in the sense that God created. Nevertheless, Adam did not try to be something other than what God created him to be. Therefore, it is important to cherish your gift because God gave it to you to help you to succeed in your assignment.

The first man was a gardener:

> *"Then the LORD God took the man and put him in the garden of Eden to tend and keep it."*
>
> [Genesis 2:15]

As Adam used his skills in Eden, he also named all the animals in the Garden. [Genesis 2:19-20] For example; if you are destined to be a cleaner, then use that ability to clean your place of worship, or wherever it will be. Do not lift yourself up and begin to think that you deserve better. Being a cleaner or a gardener is not less significant than being a 'Head of State'; both occupations require a lot of dedication and sacrifice. It really pleases God when we utilise our talents well, because they were created for a reason. In order for your talents to make a significant impact in the world, it is important to adopt humility.

Nothing good can be achieved through the spirit of pride, especially if it is something that involves God. You are a creative work of the Lord; everything about you is an exhibition of God. [Psalm 139: 14] Look how amazing you are; the way God sees you is the same way that you must see yourself. As important as you are to God, your talents must equally be important to you, and become a blessing to others. God created us all to edify one another with our gifts.

Another key method that will help you to be productive is to remain faithful to your position in Christ. It is important to wait on the Lord in the place He has appointed for you, unless you are in the wrong location. God cannot use you the way He desires if you are in the wrong place. This is because a number of believers have tried to cultivate their skills in the wrong places. Our talents cannot fully live up to their potential if we try to utilise them in environments where they cannot abound to God's glory. This can also happen when we share our talents with people who do not see their significance.

All believers are talented in various ways, but some forget the One who gave them the talents, and they end up using their skills to gain the world's applause. The world is filled with gifted individuals who were nurtured in Church. However, multitudes of believers have rejected the Kingdom and have gone into the world to do their own thing. As a matter of fact, many are convinced that they are being led by God. This is a great concern, because such individuals have removed the holiness of their gifts and replaced them with worldliness which only leads to darkness.

> *"Woe to those who go down to Egypt for help, and rely on horses, who trust in chariots because they are many, and in horsemen because they are very strong, but who do not look to the Holy One of Israel, nor seek the LORD!"*
> [Isaiah 31:1]

This is often because many believe that the Church will not help them to be the people they aspire to be, and in turn, they reach out to the world for help. Worst of all, they do not return to their first love - Christ, because they are often blinded by the wealth and recognition they receive from the world. What should be used in the Church should not be used in the world and what should be done for the Kingdom should not be done for the world. We can invite curses if we take what belongs to God and use it to please the devil. This is how we can become defiled and cast away from the presence of the Lord. As judgemental as this may seem, it is very important that we humble ourselves and use our gifts in the right places. Moreover, it is paramount that we make use of our gifts for the right reasons so that God will receive His glory.

Questions:

Why did God not permit Adam the freedom to live both inside and outside the Garden of Eden, before the fall?

Could Adam have functioned well in the Garden and maintained his closeness to God if he was often outside?

Would God have been pleased with Adam if he tried to do things his own way?

"And he said, 'I cannot return with you nor go in with you; neither can I eat bread nor drink water with you in this place. For I have been told by the word of the LORD, *'You shall not eat bread nor drink water there, nor return by going the way you came." He said to him, 'I too am a prophet as you are, and an angel spoke to me by the word of the* LORD, *saying, 'Bring him back with you to your house, that he may eat bread and drink water." (He was lying to him.) So he went back with him, and ate bread in his house, and drank water. Now it happened, as they sat at the table, that the word of the* LORD *came to the prophet who had brought him back; and he cried out to the man of God who came from Judah, saying, 'Thus says the* LORD: *'Because you have disobeyed the word of the* LORD, *and have not kept the commandment which the* LORD *your God commanded*

> *you, but you came back, ate bread, and drank water in the place of which the* Lord *said to you, 'Eat no bread and drink no water,' your corpse shall not come to the tomb of your fathers." So it was, after he had eaten bread and after he had drunk, that he saddled the donkey for him, the prophet whom he had brought back. When he was gone, a lion met him on the road and killed him. And his corpse was thrown on the road, and the donkey stood by it. The lion also stood by the corpse. "*
>
> [1 Kings 13:16-24]

The scripture referred to above tells us about an old prophet who was instructed by God not to use a certain path on his way back home, but he allowed another man to deceive him. As a result of his disobedience to God, he was killed by a lion on his way home. The prophet was not meant to be at the house of the other prophet and he was not meant to eat and sleep there either. It is important that you do not place yourself contrary to God's direct instructions to you.

This is one of the reasons why it is crucial that you allow God to take full control of your life. When you allow God to reign in your life, you will not fall on the wrong side. When you are properly positioned according to God's divine plan, you will certainly make the impact you were created to make. Also, when you place yourself where God instructs you to be, He will favour you and give you the grace to do many wonderful things that no one can imagine.

> *"Let each one remain in the same calling in which he was called. Were you called while a slave? Do not be concerned about it; but if you can be made free, rather use it. For he who is called in the* Lord *while a slave is the* Lord*'s freedman. Likewise he who is called while free is Christ's slave. You were bought at a price; do not become slaves of men. Brethren, let each one remain with God in that state in which he was called."*
>
> [1 Corinthians 7:20-24]

In serving God, it is always good to acknowledge that we are not our own. It took the pain and suffering of Christ to redeem us. Once you give your life to Christ and declare Him as your personal Lord and Saviour, then you agree that He owns you. God is the One who made us; it is essential to appreciate Him. We must do our very best to nullify every thought that would threaten to hinder the destiny God expects us to fulfil. The pain and suffering of Christ brought us the grace of God, the Holy Spirit, eternal life and so many blessings including the gifts of the Spirit. Therefore, if it means you have to experience pain to stay in your position and play your part, then stay strong and go through it. In all of this, it is necessary to remain in your place with absolute diligence, because your pain and suffering cannot be compared to what Christ went through for you.

> *"For none of us lives to himself, and no one dies to himself. For if we live, we live to the LORD; and if we die, we die to the LORD. Therefore, whether we live or die, we are the LORD's. For to this end Christ died and rose and lived again, that He might be LORD of both the dead and the living."*
>
> [Romans 14:7-9]

Self Control

The character and conduct of Jesus Christ was strictly in alignment with the Word because He was and is the Word. [John 1:1] He was psychologically and spiritually mature. There was no way that Jesus could have made a fool of Himself although some accused him of being insane; He epitomised self-control. Jesus was not puffed up and He was never prone to stepping out of line. We have the opportunity to follow in the footsteps of the Lord and learn from Him. Christ did what He was sent to do; and He did everything the way He was supposed to do it. His mind was absolutely pure because He was perfect - as was Adam when he was created. In addition, His heart was completely focused on doing the will of the Father. Our Lord Jesus Christ was very responsible and steadfast, and nothing was powerful enough to overcome Him.

Jesus was and is the original and ultimate Soldier who has never lost and will never lose a battle. When it was time to pray, He prayed. When it was time to work, He worked, and when it was time to socialise, He did it well. Jesus took three years to train the Disciples and prepared them for His ministry. He accomplished His work on earth and He went back to Heaven to intercede for us. He did not stay longer than He needed to stay. He did not spend His time in the wrong places, and He did not let things go to waste. There were plainly limits to what He was sent to do on earth, for example He did not heal everyone nor feed all the poor.

It is important to know when to start, when to finish, and how to do what you are meant to do. This is because others have also been assigned to do their part. Therefore, it is important that you do not waste your time on doing what God has not ordained you to do. Jesus did not go somewhere else to do what He was not meant to do. He did not place Himself in someone else's position. Do not be one of those believers who likes to tread upon other people's toes. Do not try to take over other people's jobs in the Kingdom of God; do not behave as if you can do it better than they can. However, do your best to be as supportive as possible. And do your very best to do what you are appointed to do in honour of God.

> "I, therefore, the prisoner of the LORD, beseech you to walk worthy of the calling with which you were called, with all lowliness and gentleness, with long-suffering, bearing with one another in love."
>
> [Ephesians 4:1-2]

Do not force yourself to become something or someone God has not made you to be. The best thing you can do is to make yourself available and God will use you in the right place and in the right way. Therefore, learn to control yourself in everything you do. Forcing yourself to be something you are not, will drain your human strength, which will only result in failure. Moreover, when you allow God to lead you, you will surely succeed. Ignorance, pride and envy are some of the reasons why Christians fail to practice self-control. These are some of the weaknesses that persuade believers to be competitive with each other.

All the same, it only brings confusion to the Kingdom. If you think you are in the wrong role in the Body of Christ, then seek God's face and find out where you belong and He will surely guide you. Allow the Holy Spirit to assist you, because you cannot do your job well in your own strength. It takes the power of God to accomplish your assignment. Do not rush and do not put pressure on yourself to be somebody you are not. It is essential that you do not use your gift as a means to receive the world's approval.

Even so, sometimes we stand back to criticise when things go wrong. It is important to understand that we will continue to fail if we do not practise humility and deliver ourselves from the spirit of hypocrisy. In this, we exhibit our weaknesses to the world, and it is also a reflection of immaturity. Ironically, we still expect God to bless us with all the benefits. This is one of the ways that some think they can mock God, forgetting that He sees everything. It is important to show accountability and do what is expected of us, and not blame, or criticise others for our own shortcomings. Jesus was always ready to face up to His responsibilities. Jesus did not expect other people to do His job for Him; He did not let others carry Him on their shoulders. However, He exhibited remarkable leadership and accountability.

It was natural for Jesus to do the will of God faithfully and effectively because He had full control of His mind. By the grace of God, we can change our fallen and broken ways to be more like Him. We can learn to control our minds and our bodies the same way Jesus did. We are being transformed and when Christ completes His work in us we will once again be like Adam.

Bearing Fruit

One of the ways to be fruitful in the Kingdom is to let your experiences be a teacher to those who may need it. There are many young people with great potential who will take your experiences on board and apply what you have learned from Christ. As the disciples obtained their spiritual education from Jesus and passed it on to others, we also have a duty to teach others what we have learned from God.

As we raise spiritual children for Christ, we hope that they will gain the maturity in due time to birth and raise spiritual children of their own; that is how the Kingdom of God will grow. It was through the training and leadership of Gamaliel that the Apostle Paul became such a great teacher of the gospel. [Acts 22:3] To this day, Paul's legacy remains a powerful inspiration to the Body of Christ across the world.

Through the Apostle Paul's influence, Timothy became one of the greatest and most prominent teachers of the Gospel. Through the great Prophet Elijah, the Prophet Elisha became a magnificent biblical and historical figure. Through king David, Solomon became a great man and a wise king over Israel. Many lives continue to be transformed today because of the wisdom and significant influence of Bible characters. The experiences and teachings of our parents, guardians and leaders gave us all a platform for growth. Equally, our mistakes and trials, temptations and celebrations, downfalls and triumphs are all vital foundations for the future of our children and their generation, so that our children will learn the difference between right and wrong.

> *"Now in the morning, as He returned to the city, He was hungry, and seeing a fig tree by the road, He came to it and found nothing on it but leaves, and said to it, 'Let no fruit grow on you ever again.' Immediately the fig tree withered away."*
>
> [Matthew 21:18-19]

Jesus cursed the fig tree because it was not bearing fruit. The fig tree was not fulfilling its purpose as the Lord intended it to; therefore, it was of no use to anyone. God did not create us just to grow leaves and be admired. The shed blood of Christ has certainly not saved us just so we can comfortably sit on our laurels. You must not allow yourself to get to a point where God will disapprove of you as Jesus did the fig tree. After all the hard work that He has done, it would be a huge shame if we fail to prove ourselves. That fig tree used all its energy to grow leaves but could not produce any fruit. Sometimes, we use all the power of our talents to produce only a tiny fraction of what we are capable of.

People come to us seeking fruit through which they may be nourished; let them not be disappointed. God is expecting every Christian to produce, to bear abundant fruit [John 15:8] and yield eternal results to His glory. Now do you wish to disappoint God?

If you plant vegetables in your garden and discover they don't produce a crop, would that make you happy? Is the teacher supposed to be overjoyed with the students who always fail to do well in class and refuse to produce good reports?

> *"Therefore I say to you, the kingdom of God will be taken from you and given to a nation bearing the fruits of it."*
> [Matthew 21:43]

The incident of the fig tree is thus also geared toward us who are children of the Lord. We have a duty to bear fruit and represent the Kingdom of God with our substance. If you are not prepared to make yourself useful to edify the Kingdom, then God may take the privilege from you and hand it over to those who are diligent enough to bear fruit that will bring glory to His name. As the Bible speaks of bearing fruit, it is essential to begin by sowing seed. However, as you sow the seed, you must make sure that the substance of the seed grows into a significant harvest. It is imperative that the seed you sow is in line with God's will. As the grace of God continues to keep you alive, you must submit to everything that God has in store for you, because it will enable you to reach the level He expects you to reach. Your productivity is essential in the Kingdom; it is a worthy goal to utilise your proficiency to make a difference in the world.

Good Preparation And Systematic Arrangement

> *"In the beginning God created the heavens and the earth. The earth was without form, and void; and darkness was on the face of the deep. And the Spirit of God was hovering over the face of the waters.*
>
> *Then God said, 'Let there be light'; and there was light and God saw the light, that it was good; and God divided the light from the darkness. God called the light Day, and the darkness He called Night. So the evening and the morning were the first day.*
>
> *Then God said, 'Let there be a firmament in the midst of the waters, and let it divide the waters from the waters.' Thus God made the firmament, and divided the waters which were under the firmament from the waters which were above the firmament; and it was so."*
>
> [Genesis 1:1-7]

In order to be a successful person, it is important to be organised and well prepared. There is never a time that God does things haphazardly. Every time the Lord does something, He does it with diligence and power. God is always precise; He remains the same at all times and He is everywhere at the same time. Therefore, it is important to do things appropriately, especially in the Kingdom business.

> *"Thus the heavens and the earth, and all the host of them, were finished, and on the seventh day God ended His work which He had done, and He rested on the seventh day from*

all His work which He had done."

[Genesis 2:1-2]

In the beginning, God used six days to create the world, and then He rested on the seventh day. God could have done it all in an instant, but He decided to maintain a progression. The Lord used one day to create the animals and He chose separate days to create other things and another day to create man. It is vital that we do things accordingly, so that nothing will fall apart. God does not make mistakes; He made things one step at a time, so that we can apply the same method whenever we embark on doing something. The six days represent the length of time - whatever period that actually is - to bring our assignments to fruition. The seventh day was the day God used to look at what He had created and saw that it was all good. Likewise, it is essential to sit back from time to time and evaluate the work we do.

As we follow this principle, we can check for errors and see if there is any room for improvement. Applying this shrewd method can certainly help us to do what is necessary and avoid what is pointless. However, when we rush and try to accomplish everything in an instant with our own strength, that is when we make terrible mistakes which often result in disappointment. Rushing into things makes it impossible for us to maintain a steady progression; being hasty does not give us the time we need to execute our plans effectively. God's mind is extremely pure and perfect. The Lord does not do anything that is detrimental, because He always follows a wise pattern. This is why everything He says and does has significance.

"And God called the firmament Heaven. So the evening and the morning were the second day. Then God said, 'Let the waters under the heavens be gathered together into one place, and let the dry land appear'; and it was so, and God called the dry land Earth, and the gathering together of the waters He called Seas, and God saw that it was good.

> *Then God said, 'Let the earth bring forth grass, the herb that yields seed, and the fruit tree that yields fruit according to its kind, whose seed is in itself, on the earth'; and it was so, and the earth brought forth grass, the herb that yields seed according to its kind, and the tree that yields fruit, whose seed is in itself according to its kind, and God saw that it was good.*
>
> [Genesis 1:8-12]

It is very important that we learn to follow suit and apply God's principles daily. God does not take too long to do things, nor is He ever hasty, but in all things, He has absolute control of Himself. It is essential to have a good reason for everything you do and it is equally important that you do it with moderation. If you live your life according to the principles of God, you will have no reason to fail.

It is plain to see how effective we can be in utilising our talents and gifts if we rely on God and apply His wisdom in everything we do. God will surely be happy to see you make good use of what He has instilled in you. Moreover, as God feels good about you, you will also be overjoyed about yourself and you will begin to look at life differently. However, when God feels disappointed in you, you will feel the same because He dwells in you. You will definitely feel what God feels and He will let you know when things are not right. Therefore, you must consider why you might be bitter about specific things in your life. It could be that God is unhappy about those particular areas of your life. This is one of the ways to know if you are not living up to your full potential. However, always bear in mind that you have the opportunity to turn things around because God is always with you to empower you.

Chapter Seven

The Power To Overcome

"For whatever is born of God overcomes the world, and this is the victory that has overcome the world - our faith."

[1 John 5:4]

Strength And Courage

It takes courage and strength to conquer, but most of all, it takes wisdom to understand the importance of conquest. Life is full of challenges that can stand in our way. Though, some are greater than others are, they can all be conquered. [Joshua 1:9] The beginning of a journey is important, but it is crucial to appreciate that the end of a journey is greater than its beginning. It takes a lot of boldness for any individual to decide to embark on a journey, especially when it seems impossible.

For a number of years, I have noticed that many Christians have remained trapped in the cages of fear and doubt. This has caused many individuals to feel inadequate and has led people into failure. Worst of all, things continue to appear impossible to such people, because their mental entrapment has persuaded them to believe that they either need to be rescued by other individuals, or they would rather die defeated. It is important to get support from another individual; the truth is that none of us has the power to make it on our own, because we all need someone to lean on. However, it is better to have the ability to stand on your own feet, because your helpers will not always be around you.

Sometimes, it is not that we lack the boldness to take the necessary action; but occasionally, it is a result of the number of obstacles that stand in our way. There are times that some obstacles seem too great to conquer; we all struggle with the temptation to give up along the way. But, those who prevail are the ones who receive their reward.

"Then Caleb quieted the people before Moses, and said, 'Let

> us go up at once and take possession, for we are well able to overcome it.'"
>
> [Numbers 13:30]

We can see that Caleb encouraged the Israelites to be strong. He made them aware that they had the power to conquer the land of the giants because the people were afraid to do so. Caleb's encouragement gave the people the confidence they needed to overcome their enemies.

The friends of the paralysed man in the New Testament made an opening in the roof above where Jesus was teaching in order to lower him into His presence to receive healing. The roof was a hindrance, but they did not allow it to remain an interference for long. In fact, the men exhibited courage and took charge. They created the opportunity to achieve their goal. The men succeeded because they realised that their goal was more significant than their obstacle. [Mark 2:4]

> "Have I not commanded you? Be strong and of good courage; do not be afraid, nor be dismayed, for the LORD your God is with you wherever you go."
>
> [Joshua 1:9]

Joshua did not know that God was going to call him to lead the children of Israel into the Promised Land. Though there were others more experienced than he was, God chose Joshua to follow in the footsteps of Moses. Joshua took on the role without questioning God and he accepted it with humility and all diligence. [Joshua 1:1-5]

Question:

What does God do when He is about to call you on a mission?

It is important to understand that the work of God is great. It is not difficult to see that great things always come with great responsibilities. God commanded Joshua to be strong and courageous because it takes a lot of boldness to work for the Lord.

When God appoints you, it provokes your enemies, and you will need God's protection in order to complete your assignment. Do not be afraid to acknowledge that your talent is a blessing; cherish it with all your heart and all your strength. The substance in you is more precious than anyone can ever imagine.

No one can take away our valour, because it is God who made us. Yet, we can cower in fear and fail to exercise bold faith. We cannot be who God created us to be if we continue to be gutless. Therefore, let us believe in the Lord and trust that He will never fail nor forsake us.

Confront And Conquer

> *"And the king and his men went to Jerusalem against the Jebusites, the inhabitants of the land, who spoke to David, saying, 'You shall not come in here; but the blind and the lame will repel you,' thinking, 'David cannot come in here.'"*
>
> [2 Samuel 5:6]

According to this, we can see that the Jebusites tried to prevent king David from entering the city of Jerusalem. The Jebusites were a great hindrance to king David and his men. However, David stood firm and took over their great city. The Bible does not state how long it took David to conquer the Jebusites. It could have been days, weeks, months or years. Nevertheless, we have the record of king David's triumphant entry into the city of Jerusalem; he was not afraid of the Jebusites. Though, they were a seemingly insurmountable challenge, David did what was necessary to possess their city. [2 Samuel 5:7-8] The scripture explains how David made his way into the city to take possession of it. Similarly, you too can push through and conquer regardless of how difficult things appear to be. That same city became well known as 'The City of David'. Jerusalem would not have that name if David allowed the threats of the Jebusites to discourage him. When you are relentless like David, you will attain your prize which will bear your name.

> *"So David went on and became great, and the LORD God of hosts was with him. Then Hiram king of Tyre sent messengers to David, and cedar trees, and carpenters and masons. And they built David a house."*
> [2 Samuel 5:10-11]

Notice in the above Bible passage that king David grew stronger and became a great man. He obtained the favour of the people and reverence from another king. Many servants were at his disposal to build a house for him because of his victorious endeavour. Apart from that, David received more favour from the Lord who established him as king over that land. [2 Samuel 7:26-27] Greatness is a reward for those who are prepared to fight for their purpose. Through king David's experience, God is telling us all to trust in Him and take this wonderful opportunity to stand firm in the midst of every difficult situation. The Bible passage is an assurance from God to help you understand that He is always with you to make sure that you never lose a fight in your life. It is clear that without God, it is impossible to win any battle at all. Therefore, be confident in the Lord with all your heart all the days of your life.

Fight The Good Fight Of Faith

> *"Fight the good fight of faith, lay hold on eternal life, to which you were also called and have confessed the good confession in the presence of many witnesses."*
> [1 Timothy 6:12]

The Bible passage really helped me to stay strong in the Lord when circumstances came to challenge me. Although Paul had great challenges, he continued to focus on his calling. He stood firm like a mighty pillar and triumphed over all his trials, because he passionately lived for Christ. Eventually, he prevailed since the Lord was with him and he confidently declared that he had fought a good fight. *"I have fought the good fight, I have finished the race, I have kept the faith."*. [2 Timothy 4:7]

Paul gained victory because he relied on the power of God. In addition, he testified that he kept the faith and finished his course. He fought hard and well indeed. May God give you the power to finish your course. As long as God is alive, you can also fight the good fight and keep the faith.

Considering the many false allegations against Paul, he remained solid on his feet throughout, as the grace of God enabled him to stand strong. In addition, he was wrongfully arrested and imprisoned. Paul was threatened by some powerful enemies who opposed him. Also, the great apostle was confronted by many near-death situations, such as being bitten by a poisonous snake, facing a death sentence, being in a shipwreck and being trapped in the ocean for several hours. [Acts 23:11]

Let us not forget the thirty-nine lashes he received five times from people who hated him. [2 Corinthians 11:24] Nevertheless, this apostle of God prevailed at all costs and he testified of the Lord as a way of encouraging Timothy and Christians down the ages. [2 Timothy 4:7] This means that Paul did not allow his challenges to deter him from the faith, but he fulfilled his destiny because of his relentless commitment to Christ. If Paul had chosen to compromise, there is a possibility that he would have failed to finish his calling in the Lord. Even so, this powerful testimony of Paul is one of the greatest platforms for all Christians to use as a stepping-stone to finish their course. Just as Paul overcame the false accusations that he received from his enemies, you too can overcome every challenge in your life. [Acts 25:7-11]

Our experiences are like great ships that carry others by virtue of inspiring them to make similar journeys in their own lives. We are privileged that our legacies become significant tools to educate and strengthen those who are in need of guidance and inspiration. It was the powerful testimonies of our mothers and fathers that have brought many of us through difficulties and continue to help us. Therefore, without the benefit of knowing our history, many of our children could fall behind and probably go astray without any hope.

> *"I press toward the goal for the prize of the upward call of God in Christ Jesus."*
> [Philippians 3:14]

It will be impossible for you to be great if you are often afraid of challenges that oppose you. If you are hungry enough and prepared to go the extra mile, then victory will be in the palm of your hands. Therefore, remember that your purpose is much greater than your challenges. The amount and the weight of obstacles in your way do not matter, what matters is that God is with you and He will never forsake you. Regardless of how powerful your circumstances appear to be, you can make it if you settle your trust in God. You will surely conquer as long as you abide in God. Remember what the Bible says about you; remind yourself each day that *"you are more than a conqueror"* [Romans 8:37] and are *"fearfully and wonderfully made"*. [Psalm 139:14]

It is evident through Paul's experience that trusting in God is the most fruitful choice to make. It is only through the power of God that we can all prevail and triumph against all odds. I have learned a lot from Paul's experience. It has strengthened me indeed and brought me closer to God. In addition, it is gradually helping me to be transformed into the image of Christ. Even if your faith is as small as a minute grain of sand, God can use that tiny faith and turn it into a remarkable history. As long as the Lord is by your side, you will never be ashamed.

The Victory In Humility And The Defeat In Pride

There are certain things that often hinder us from achieving the goals that are set before us. Pride, ignorance, bitterness, anger, idolatry and other weaknesses are many of the things that prevent us from receiving the blessings of the Lord. Sometimes we think we are so strong that we actually believe we can handle anything on our own until we experience the harsh reality.

> *"Therefore let him who thinks he stands take heed lest he fall."*
>
> [1 Corinthians 10:12

Do not be a self-made hero; you must be careful not to think of yourself as the best Christian in your church or the most invincible person in your neighbourhood. You must not imagine that you are more spiritual or wiser than others. Jesus condemned this attitude in the Pharisees. As much as they were God-fearing, their mentality and disposition was contrary to the principles of Christ. This was a result of their distorted values. The Pharisees and the Sadducees allowed their ignorance to guide them, and this made it difficult for them to bring about the necessary change. [Mark 12:38-40] Change only surfaced when Jesus came to reveal their wrongdoings and showed them the right way. It is not about impressing others with how much you know or how experienced you think you are. When you lift your head up too high and place the most expensive price-tag on your head and look down on others as if they are nothing, God will cast you down to the point at which you again humble yourself before Him. [1 Samuel 15]

> *"The fear of man brings a snare, but whoever trusts in the LORD shall be safe. Many seek the ruler's favour, but justice for man comes from the LORD."*
>
> [Proverbs 29:25-26]

The devil always aims to place us in situations that only cause us to lose focus; he will try his best to get you to pay attention to yourself. He can and will try to use another individual to derail you from your walk with God, so that you will fail to be an overcomer. Sometimes, it can be difficult to receive certain blessings from God if you are distracted by anger, money, jealousy, envy and the like. Many of us are dramatically failing to achieve goals that God has set for us because we often refuse to accept the fact that the road to success will not always be smooth. Some individuals grew up in privileged environments which often sheltered them from disaster. Therefore, they may not fully have the understanding and the expertise to confront difficult situations.

Sometimes, things turn out that way because their upbringing did not make room for any type of disciplined preparation. Some also believe it is not their duty to be responsible, so they continue to be conceited. This attitude causes them to think that it is alright to subsist on other people's efforts and not their own. Others refuse to admit it when they are wrong, as they are not often told when they say or do things inappropriately. Thus, they tend to cast blame upon others and cause offence when things go wrong, even when they know they have made an error. Also, they try to prove their point by cooking up clever excuses to cover their faults and expect others to agree with them. These are also the types who love to put themselves in a position to correct others but they refuse to accept good counsel, especially because they think they know it all. We should not expect others to comply with our views if we cannot humble ourselves enough to receive the advice of others.

There are also those who refuse to change because they strongly believe that they are automatically inerrant; and thus refuse to accept correction. We cannot force people to change if we are not prepared to set good examples ourselves. Some even go as far as destroying the lives of others in order to gain what they want; this sort of behaviour is causing many believers to fall further behind and lose the battle.

Some, possibly, did not have anyone to teach them, so they grew up without any spiritual wisdom, discretion, or any sense of direction. Others have been led astray by the influence of the world. These are some of the things that frequently prevent us from stepping into our 'promised land' to possess our milk and honey. We must repent and make room for significant change in order to overcome the wiles of the enemy.

It is wise to be careful of the type of associations you have. There are certain friends who are a potential danger to your walk in Christ and you must be fully aware of how they influence you. It is very unsafe to involve yourself in things that will only lead to damnation. It is not wise for children of God to engage in ungodly activities. We should avoid these things which are diametrically against what Christ stands for. Some believers are failing to overcome because they are deeply involved in ungodly relationships which continue to make their lives miserable, but they are too involved and too comfortable to notice or understand the reason for the difficulties they face. These are some of the choices we make, which prohibit us from receiving the blessings of the Lord and so become the champions we were created to be.

It is essential that we courageously demonstrate the necessary judgments in order to relinquish all the negative things that can potentially destroy us. We must disassociate ourselves from activities that only cause us to fall into darkness. It is imperative that we do our best to be as humble as possible in order to bring glory to God.

> *"But also for this very reason, giving all diligence, add to your faith virtue, to virtue knowledge, to knowledge self-control, to self-control perseverance, to perseverance godliness, to godliness brotherly kindness, and to brotherly kindness love."*
> [2 Peter 1:5-7]

As we humble ourselves in the presence of the Lord, our lives will begin to change for the better. As we bow before God, *"He will work all things together for our good."* [Romans 8:28] Such is the way forward; humility will empower us to overcome, but pride will strip us of the strength we need to triumph.

Chapter Eight

Prudence

"I, wisdom, dwell with prudence, and find out knowledge and discretion.
[Proverbs 8:12]

The Definition

In order to be well established in life, it is very important to have a healthy understanding of prudence. It is essential to make good use of the little you have. [Matthew 15:34] It does not matter how small your beginnings, your diligence will determine your destiny.

There are many ways to describe the essence of prudence - being cautious, able to evaluate things, shrewd, wise, practical, and having good sense. Conversely prudence is the opposite of recklessness or lack of common sense. It is often said that the ant is a prudent creature because it always prepares things in advance before winter. Reckless people are individuals who do not take time to consider what is ahead of them, but often squander what they have as if the world has already come to an end. Therefore, a prudent person is someone who thinks ahead and does things meticulously.

When the word 'prudence' is mentioned, it is often associated with money. However, it is important to acknowledge that there are many other ways that we can practice it.

For example, we can be prudent with our words; if we think and gather ourselves properly before we speak, life would be easier for us.

Another way to be prudent is to know your limit; for example, do not exceed the amount of possessions you acquire because too many items in your life could be a great hindrance. You can also be prudent by watching what you eat and what you drink, especially if it is often in excess. You can be prudent with your time and the activities in your life.

Perhaps, you spend too much time with your friends and not enough time with yourself. Maybe, you put too much effort in certain areas of your life, but you are very neglectful in other parts that could dramatically improve if you use your time proficiently. You can be prudent with your sleep and you can be prudent with the things you occupy yourself with. This is most important, if you are often caught up in numerous events at the same time. Sometimes, circumstances can prevent us from getting enough sleep and rest, especially when issues become too catastrophic. This is how many people have become depressed and despondent.

Jesus Christ was a master of prudence because He always applied that principle in everything He did. God is the epitome of prudence; He does things with consideration. When God created the world, He used the attribute of prudence. Likewise, He uses prudence to relate to us by being patient with us. He does not handle us recklessly, but He is ever gracious with us. This tells us that patience is a form of prudence because it gives us the time to gather our thoughts properly before we make a decision. In life, it is evident that people who are often impatient only make matters worse for themselves as well as others. Impatience has caused many disasters; it has destroyed great establishments and has brought pain to multitudes of people.

Now when the people saw that Moses delayed coming down from the mountain, the people gathered together to Aaron, and said to him:

> *"Come, make us gods that shall go before us; for as for this Moses, the man who brought us up out of the land of Egypt, we do not know what has become of him."*
>
> [Exodus 32:1]

We see that as the Israelites became impatient with Moses' absence, they pressured Aaron to fashion an idol for them. They would not wait for their Moses to return from his meeting with God. The people could have remained calm for a little longer and remained loyal to Moses, but they became reckless because they failed to take all things into consideration. Through their lack of thoughtfulness, they carelessly lost their way and fell back into sin. Choosing to worship an idol brought judgement upon them and some 3,000 died that day. [Exodus 32:28] This is how far lack of prudence can take you. Failure to be prudent can actually produce consequences. When you calculate things properly, it means you are being prudent. When you only spend what you need to spend and save the rest, then you are being prudent. When you only attain what is profitable and ignore what is irrelevant, then it means - you are being prudent. When you do not rush into things, it means you are being prudent. I say this because lack of contentment can cause an individual to become reckless like the children of Israel.

Excessive Spending

There is a story of a wealthy man who purchased a mansion for his wife just because she wanted one. The couple already shared a beautiful mansion which contained everything they needed. They lived a very comfortable life and did not struggle for anything. But, after the man bought his wife the house, she left it empty - as she was too busy to spend time in it. In addition, she persuaded her husband to employ staff to maintain it for her sake. Even after a couple of years had gone by, the woman was only able to visit the mansion a few times because it was just a second home for her. Not long after that, the man told his wife that he was going to sell the house in order to cut back on spending. He had to do that because he began to experience some financial difficulties. However, the woman was not happy as she realised that she was going to lose the mansion. Her lack of prudence could have resulted in bankruptcy. Furthermore, she could have relented from persuading her husband to purchase the mansion in the first place, especially as she did not intend to use it as an investment.

The mansion could have been used to generate more income for the family. The man sat his wife down and explained that the bills were more than enough to feed an entire family for several years. Plus, the cost of paying the staff for maintenance purposes was enough to build three luxurious homes. Apart from that, the man calculated the expenses he accrued from the amount of parties his wife held at the mansion. Also, the man added the cost of furniture and decorations.

Did the woman really need another mansion? All the money that was wasted could have been utilised profitably. This, is why it is important to distinguish between our wants and our needs. [1 Timothy 6:10] The things we possess can become burdensome if they are of no use to us. It is very unwise to have assets that will only satisfy our ego. I once watched a documentary about a wealthy man who had about ten luxurious vehicles in his driveway, but he did not have anywhere to go. Being wealthy is not an excuse to be wasteful; wealth requires wisdom, humility and accountability.

Gather Your Crumbs

> *"So when they were filled, He said to His disciples, 'Gather up the fragments that remain, so that nothing is lost.'"*
> [John 6:12-1]

After Jesus fed the five thousand, He told His disciples to gather up the fragments, which filled twelve bags. Gather those little fragments in your life - whether they be money, food, possessions, or the like. Those little fragments will add more years to your life.

Pharaoh had a dream of a serious famine that was to occur for a period of seven years. Pharaoh complied with Joseph's advice as he interpreted the dream. In addition, Pharaoh instructed his people to store up as much food as possible in order to survive the disaster.

There is the possibility that many people who were less

fortunate must have died from the famine, but Pharaoh's Egyptian household was clothed in abundance. The dream was a red alert from God to help the land; it gave the nation plenty of time to prepare themselves to face the situation. [Genesis 41]

If you hold up a glass under a tap and the tap yields only drops of water, the glass will eventually become full. Because of the wait, you will cherish it more. If the tap rapidly runs full of water, then there is a possibility that, it could overflow over the glass too quickly and go to waste. The reason for this is that, if the tap runs at an appropriate speed, then the flow of water can be monitored. This also means that impurities in the water can be spotted and removed in time. If the water runs too fast, then it will be difficult to monitor and control.

When something is out of control, it often leaves little room for improvement, especially when it happens without warning. Likewise, Pharaoh's dream was like looking through the glass of water, because he saw the catastrophe in advance, and through Joseph's advice, he was able to keep things under control. This helped the nation of Egypt to live in peace and abundance during the occurrence of the great famine. It is imperative to keep track of, and control the flow of issues in your life. Learn to identify what is pertinent and what is not. The unwanted crumbs in your life may one day be your most precious treasure.

Money Matters

When it comes to money, put yourself in the place of an unwanted penny; the penny that is often kicked across the street, because it seems embarrassing to pick it up in public. That common dirty penny is very special, because there is much profit in it. Such is the Kingdom of God: it is full of sinners whom the world always rejects, but the grace of God comes and locates them all. God washes them all together and then before long, the rest of the world can see the shining glory of the Lord upon them. We do not have to look like angels or be like them for God to accept us; He created us and loved us from the beginning. People often pay more attention to the shiny coins and reject the dirty pennies. We were all like dirty pennies before God, but He still sent His only begotten Son to shed His blood for us, because He only focused on the preciousness in us. [John 15:13] Sometimes, the best things in life are things that were once broken, but after being fixed, became even better than before.

> *"I have given them Your Word; and the world has hated them because they are not of the world, just as I am not of the world."*
>
> [John 17:14]

Many people have been affected negatively because the world has treated them like unwanted pennies. However, God loves those whom the world oppresses; they are the foundations of the future. This is why God always polishes sinners and transforms their lives. The ones whom the world tries to destroy; those who are often cast out by the ignorance and selfishness of the world, do not remain weak for long, because persecution is only for a season. Sometimes, those who put pennies in the offering basket become a laughingstock as a result of ignorance. Some do not regard that pocket change as real money because they fail to see the substance in that type of currency. It is not about who has the thickest wad of cash or the biggest bank account, but it is all about God and what He says.

> *"In these lay a great multitude of sick people, blind, lame, paralyzed, waiting for the moving of the water. For an angel went down at a certain time into the pool and stirred up the water; then whoever stepped in first, after the stirring of the water, was made well of whatever disease he had.*
>
> *Now a certain man was there who had an infirmity thirty-eight years. When Jesus saw him lying there, and knew that he already had been in that condition a long time, He*

> *said to him, 'Do you want to be made well?'*
>
> *The sick man answered Him, 'Sir, I have no man to put me into the pool when the water is stirred up; but while I am coming, another steps down before me.' Jesus said to him, 'Rise, take up your bed and walk.'*
> *And immediately the man was made well, took up his bed, and walked. And that day was the Sabbath. The Jews therefore said to him who was cured, 'It is the Sabbath; it is not lawful for you to carry your bed.' He answered them, "He who made me well said to me, 'Take up your bed and walk.'"*
>
> [John 5:3-11]

Isn't God amazing! He is ready to save all, polish all, and renew all; God is not wasteful, because we are all precious to Him. God has absolute wisdom and He makes use of everything He creates because He has good plans for all things. Think of the word 'Saviour'. The Lord is our Saviour, because He saves all and He does not waste a single soul.

Put your mind on Christ today and begin to see any surplus in your life as the foundations to your future. All the unwanted possessions in your life comprise the key to your harvest. Save all that you can save, sell those old clothes and those old shoes that you have selfishly kept in your closet for so long. [See John 6:44-45]

All the remnants of food that you throw away each day could be useful. It is unprofitable to spend so much on items that you are just going to keep in your cabinet. You can save that money for the seasons of famine, so that you and your generation will be blessed. You may even be able to assist your neighbours who are in need.

Take another look at all your basic assets by looking at your children. They are all the same in the sense that they are valuable seeds that need to be wisely cultivated until they grow in stature ready to face the world. God has given us

His wisdom and understanding as the keys to prosperity; therefore, it is lucrative to be prudent. [Proverbs 2:6]

> *"Understanding is a wellspring of life to him who has it.*
> *But the correction of fools is folly."*
> [Proverbs 16:22]

Understanding will give you the patience to endure as you save. Also, it will help you to turn your little hills into a mountain. It is not easy to be patient in a world that is so quick and impulsive, but the wisdom of God can keep your feet on solid ground regardless of the occurrences around you. As Jesus spoke the parable of the five talents, the significant point was about making use of the smallest things that God puts in your life. God has declared in His Word that we should not lean on our own understanding; what we see is not what God sees. Every seed God puts in your hand already contains a harvest. But, it is your responsibility to cultivate it until it bears good fruit.

Sperm and egg are so small that the human eye cannot perceive. But, by the mystery of God, they come together and eventually form a baby. After the baby is born, he or she becomes a toddler, then after a number of years – a teenager, then a full grown adult. Every human being arises from a minute amount of substance until we all become, in effect, Giants. That is why sometimes, when we see a little baby, we say things such as *"He will be a lawyer"* or *"She will be a nurse"* or *"It looks as if this one will be a Pastor or a Prophet"*. We often speak of young children as if we already know the end-result, particularly when we imagine the babies as adults. Likewise, whenever God blesses us with something, it is important that we do not focus too much on the size of the gift, because everything that comes from God has the potential to multiply beyond our wildest imagination.

Whatever you do, do not belittle anything that God blesses you with - even if it appears to be insignificant. The size of the seed in the palm of your hand does not matter; it is not what you think or what you perceive that matters. But, what is important is the aftermath. Once you put that little penny in your savings account, it begins to accumulate interest. In doing so, it will grow into a greater amount. One seed alone can proliferate and become a forest; a penny can become a million. Therefore, be prudent.

Final Word

As the words in this book have passed through your eyes and penetrated your soul, may you experience the transformative power of God's Word. You may not be the most popular individual in your neighbourhood. Nevertheless, I believe this book will turn you from a timid to a warrior 'Gideon' capable of conquering great enemies. Perhaps, you are overwhelmed by some habits that seem impossible to shake off. I trust that this book, which is inspired by the Holy Ghost, has helped you to discover your potential to conquer all those things that have impeded your progress so far.

Perhaps, you have some unique ideas that have the potential to transform the world into a better place, but you lack the correct guidance to make effective use of them. I pray that all you have learned from this book will point you in the right direction and into greener pastures. As you have read this book, may every crooked path in your life become straight. May every confusion be erased and every lack of progress be reversed into advancement. May you excel in your purpose and move forward from glory to glory, in the name of Jesus. God bless you.

Also By The Author

The Ark, The Flood and The Rainbow

The story of Noah's flood is commonly known throughout the world. However, our focus is all too often on a boat, rain and the animals and in so doing, we miss the deeper meanings and message of this remarkable account of God's Salvation.

In 'The Ark, The Flood and The Rainbow', Isaac challenges us to look again and look more closely at the Biblical text to understand what God is trying to tell us. The world has taken the story of Noah for granted and watered it down for too long. In fact, it is often perceived as a man-made story for children. However, Isaac dares to challenge and remove the myth about The Ark, The Flood and The Rainbow in order to unveil the Divine truth which has been misunderstood for centuries.

This book will take you on a journey to realisation and enlightenment about the will of God, the love of God and the power of God.

ISBN 978-1-90797-108-2

Available from www.jesusjoypublishing.co.uk

www.ingramcontent.com/pod-product-compliance
Lightning Source LLC
Chambersburg PA
CBHW061652040426
42446CB00010B/1698